13. Elma's home on Radičević St.
14. Eternal Flame
15. Markale
16. Vaso Miskin St.
17. Drvenija Bridge

18. Jewish Community Centre
19. National Library
20. Brewery
21. Elma's parents' home

Sarajevo Days,
Sarajevo Nights

Sarajevo Days, Sarajevo Nights

Elma Softić

Translated by Nada Conić

 Hungry Mind Press

First U.S. Edition
Published by Hungry Mind Press
57 Macalester Street
Saint Paul, Minnesota 55105

Published in the United States of America
by arrangement with
Key Porter Books, Ltd.
Toronto, Ontario
Canada

9   8   7   6   5   4   3   2   1
First Hungry Mind Press printing, 1996

Library of Congress catalog number: 96-76409
ISBN: 1-886913-10-2

Printed in the United States of America

Cover design: Scott Richardson

The publishers gratefully acknowledge Colonel Matt Macdonald and Major Rita Lepage of the Canadian Armed Forces, for conveying sections of this manuscript out of Sarajevo.

Translator's Preface:
Parallel Lives

Until the spring of 1992, when she was thirty, Elma Softić led a relatively happy, middle-class life. She lived with her parents and her younger sister Ilona, taught philosophy at a business college, enjoyed the cafe life of a cosmopolitan city, and indulged her tastes for science fiction, fashion magazines, pastries, and "golden oldies" music. Her proudest moment was during the '84 Winter Olympics in Sarajevo, when she skated as one of the four "Wolfie" mascots at the closing ceremonies of the games. (She was also one of the Bosnian figure-skating judges at that time.)

It was on Orthodox Good Friday, 1994, that I first "met" Elma, here in Toronto, through a photocopied text of her letters. A literary agent from Zagreb had shown up at a publishing house with a manuscript of Elma's letters – unfortunately, untranslated. At first I was skeptical: all too often, people in interesting and significant places have nothing either interesting or significant to say. Then I began to read: Sarajevo, Elma wrote, was like a chained circus elephant, shifting aimlessly from side to side, his existence meaningless and demeaned. The vividness and intensity of her writing leapt off the page. I immediately volunteered to translate sample passages: I was determined not to let anyone else take this task away from me. Elma would be my eyes and ears in this war, and I would be her English voice.

I feel a deeper empathy with Elma than my Canadian birth and upbringing would suggest. My father, a Serb, had been an officer in Draža Mihailović's Chetnik army and a prisoner of war of the Nazis; my Slovene mother had been sent by the Nazis to work as slave labour on an Austrian farm for a year, and like Elma, she had spent years running from bombs and

1

hiding in basements. Since the summer of 1991, when Slovenia declared its independence from (by then) Serb-ruled Yugoslavia, and federal jets bombed it in retaliation, my father's people attacking my mother's homeland, I too have been a captive, helpless but fascinated, of the bloody, bewildering drama of this most recent Balkan war. I had been reared on stories of that other war, like the present one, a blend of international *realpolitik*, factional strife, and competing mythologies. The battles of Partizans and Chetniks were refought over our family dinner table, and I intuitively understood the dilemma of the present-day Bosnians, unwilling to take sides and yet pressured to choose, wishing both to keep it all and to have none of it. So I felt an immediate kinship with Elma, whose father is Muslim and mother Jewish, though her childhood experience was quite different.

World War II did not loom large in her consciousness. Her parents were largely silent about it, even though her mother had lost most of her maternal relatives in the Holocaust and some of her paternal ones in the Chetnik massacre of the Muslims in Foča in 1941. Both of Elma's parents avoided ethnic and religious labels, identifying themselves merely as "Yugoslavs" in the census. The family clearly had both a faith and a stake in Tito's slogan of "brotherhood and unity" among the various nations making up Yugoslavia. This has been a reality as well as an ideal for Elma: her friends and neighbours included Serbs and Croats as well as Muslims and Jews. They still do.

Yet the aspiration to universality is always in conflict with the longing for a particular identity. Secular and atheist, Elma ignored her Jewishness until 1982. That was the year of the Israeli raid on the Sabra and Shatila refugee camps in southern Lebanon, in which Palestinian civilians were massacred. While at a pro-Palestinian rally protesting the raid, she saw a placard bearing the slogan "Alle Juden schiessen!" *[Shoot all Jews]*. For her, it was a mirror in which she suddenly saw herself as a Jew.

For Elma, diversity is a value and a necessity, the condition of her acceptance in the larger community. Yet this ideal has been, along with truth, an early casualty, indeed a deliberate target, of this war.

The reader may understandably ask at this point for an "unbiased" explanation of this war – "just the facts, ma'am...." Unfortunately, this is difficult for several reasons. First, one cannot even name this war without "taking sides," because it is in part a war over names and interpretations. For instance, is it a civil war or a war of foreign aggression? The Bosnian government argues (as does Elma, of course) that it is a war of aggression: the Yugoslav National Army (the federal army of the former Yugoslavia, now under the command of the "rump state" of Serbia and Montenegro) and Chetnik irregulars from Serbia have armed, supplied, and fought alongside Bosnian Serbs from the beginning, and indeed, were primarily responsible for the ethnic cleansing of eastern Bosnia in 1992, *after* Bosnia-Herzegovina* declared independence on March 3. This aggression is a fact; though the "Yugoslav" and Bosnian Serbs strenuously denied it for years, it was an open secret, amply confirmed by journalists and intelligence reports, that is now generally admitted by Western governments. On the other hand, Serbia-Montenegro has never recognized the sovereignty of BiH; from Serbian president Milošević's point of view, it is an internal matter. One cannot remain neutral on this point. And as a matter of fact, Europe and the United Nations took sides at the very beginning of the war by officially recognizing BiH, on April 6 and May 22, respectively. In the following months, economic sanctions were imposed on Serbia and Montenegro, and their claim to the former Yugoslavia's seat in the UN was rejected. The London Conference in August condemned ethnic cleansing and affirmed the sovereignty and territorial integrity of BiH. This has been the official position of the UN ever since. Though the Bosnian Serbs led by Radovan Karadžić declared the "Serb Republic of Bosnia"** on March 27, 1992, it has never been recognized by the international community.

Cyrus Vance and David Owen, special envoys of the UN and the European Community, respectively, were assigned the task of designing a peace plan on the basis of these "facts" and principles. What they proceeded to propose was as astonishing to me as it was to Elma. The Vance-Owen

---

*Henceforth, BiH [Bosnia i (=and) Herzegovina], its official acronym.
**Its "parliament" meets in the "capital," Pale, a former ski resort about seventeen kilometres east of Sarajevo.

peace plan consisted of the division of BiH into a loose confederation of nine "ethnic cantons," three each for Serbs, Croats, and Muslims, and a tenth, multi-ethnic canton of Sarajevo under UN supervision, rather like Berlin after World War II. At least 50,000 UN peacekeeping troops would be needed, probably indefinitely, to police this unviable state. It was, essentially, a colonial solution, similar to the division of India and Pakistan, an analogy not lost on Elma. Moreover, in order to create the cantons, BiH and the UN would have to displace whole populations.

To Lord Owen's surprise and indignation, the Bosnian government objected to this dismemberment along tribal lines and the surrender of its own multi-ethnic principles. He complained of the recalcitrance of the "Muslim faction" (the Bosnian government was now reduced to the status of a "faction," one of the "warring parties" between whom there was nothing to choose). To put pressure on the Bosnian president, Alija Izetbegović, he approached Mate Boban, leader of the Croats of Herzegovina, and Fikret Abdić, a Muslim secessionist from the northwestern Bosnian city of Bihač – another colonial tactic. This led to the breakup of the Croat-Muslim alliance, and for the first half of 1993, the Bosnian government forces (of which the second-in-command as well as 30% of the soldiers were Serbian, by the way) had to battle not only Bosnian Serbs and their allies from Serbia but also Boban's Croat and Abdić's Muslim forces. Owen continued to insist that the government of BiH bow to the reality of Serb military superiority and their occupation of 70% of the country, or, as he put it, "the facts on the ground." In other words, Izetbegović ought to accept defeat. The "peace plan" was in fact a plan for Bosnian surrender. (Izetbegović did eventually sign, as did Karadžić, but the plan was rejected by the Bosnian Serb parliament in Pale in May 1993.)

The international community has in effect agreed with the Serbs that peaceful coexistence of the various nationalities is impossible. The Balkans, we hear repeatedly, is a site of "ancient hatreds"; this war is an inevitable consequence of World War II or the five centuries of Ottoman domination or a propensity for violence inherent in the South Slav psyche. It is essential to understand that even for men like Karadžić, the statement that coexistence is impossible is less a statement of fact than a threat and a prophecy.* Propaganda, systematic terror, mass rape, and other atrocities make it true. By accepting this statement, the West is also helping to fulfill it.

On the other hand, the Bosnian government of Alija Izetbegović, along with ordinary citizens like Elma, were committed to the vision of a multi-ethnic democracy. Naturally, though naively, they believed that the West would champion their cause. The West's failure to do so has generated among them a bitterness of which the consequences are as yet incalculable.

Despite an understandable reluctance to be "the world's policeman," Americans do have a stake in the region. The United States has been responsible for several initiatives in the Balkans, including Clinton's "lift and strike" policy which fell afoul of his European allies, and most recently, the peace accords reached in Dayton, Ohio, in November, 1995. In fact, the success of these accords seems to depend on American willingness to enforce them.

The initial U.S. reaction to the fragmentation of Yugoslavia was to support the central government, which was controlled by nationalist Serbs, notably Slobodan Milošević, against the secessionists. This was understandable, given America's own history, but unfortunately, Milošević was no Lincoln. In fact, he is generally acknowledged to be the mastermind behind "ethnic cleansing" and the whole course of the war.

Meanwhile, in the midst of this war, the UN resolved to send humanitarian aid convoys to besieged civilians, mainly Bosnian Muslims. These convoys were often stopped and the aid confiscated by the various armies and militias. (Sieges are, after all, a time-honoured method of starving the enemy into submission. Why would a besieging army consent to having its military objective thwarted by an outside party?) Accordingly, UNPROFOR, the United Nations Protection Force, was sent to various cities to ensure that the aid got through. They were initially welcomed by

---

*"Radovan Karadžić is the greatest genius Bosnia has ever produced. He says something that at the time is a complete lie. And two years later it becomes the truth." – Sarajevo law professor Zdravko Grebo, quoted by David Rieff.

the Bosnian populace, who mistakenly assumed that they had come to protect *them*. In fact, they were authorized to fire only if they themselves were fired upon. The mandate of UNPROFOR turned out to be appeasement. Friendly relations with the Serbs, it was argued, were necessary to secure the safe passage of aid convoys.

In November 1995, in Dayton, Ohio, another peace plan was signed by Izetbegović, Croatian President Franjo Tudjman, and Serbian President Slobodan Milošević. It, too, is an attempt to square the circle of contradictory demands for a united BiH and ethnic separatism. A weak central government will preside over two parliaments, one for Serb Bosnia (49% of the territory) and the other for the Muslim-Croat federation (51%). This plan requires a NATO implementation force (IFOR) of 60,000 ground troops, including 20,000 Americans, who are to return home in December, 1996. Another provision of the Dayton accords was the reunification of Sarajevo under Bosnian government control as a symbol of multi-ethnic coexistence. The transfer of Serb-occupied suburbs was completed in March 1996, under a dark cloud – of distrust and arson. Terrorized by extremist propaganda and by gangs of thugs, both Serbian and Muslim, the majority of the Serbian population abandoned the city, leaving their houses burning behind them. Reunification has not meant reconciliation.

One of the cruellest aspects of this extraordinarily cruel war is the blend of sophisticated technology and primitive brutality. Elma vividly describes the real "facts on the ground," the barbaric conditions of life in a besieged city, in which people cook over cardboard fires, shit into plastic bags, and queue up for the table scraps of UN soldiers. These are the real and tragic consequences of the international diplomatic farce. On the other hand, she has a modern education and access to international media and telecommunications. Bosnia can watch its own destruction on television. How can Elma, who has been both a student and a teacher of philosophy, survive the absurdity of such a situation?

Writing diaries and letters has helped her keep her sanity and focus. She began to keep a diary in the spring of 1992, when the fighting reached Bosnia and her life turned upside down. In the diary, she described the chaos, the terror, the denial of the fact that her old world was gone for-

6

ever. For a few months, she, her younger sister, Ilona, and her parents became "internal refugees," as they left their apartment on the exposed hillside of Alifakovac* and moved in with her grandmother downtown. Over the next several months, as the shelling continued, they became accustomed to it, lost their horror of it, ceased even to notice it at times. Eventually, they returned to their home on Alifakovac. As war became a routine, its element of surprise gone, Elma became bored and frustrated with her diary: she needed an audience. She found one through the Jewish Community Centre in Sarajevo, which maintains regular ham radio contact with its Zagreb counterpart. Her new friends in Zagreb, whom she had never met in person, urged her to send them letters. These letters created something of a sensation – people were reading them to their friends, who in turn were begging for copies – and soon found their way into newspapers and radio programs in Croatia. Eventually, the combined letters and diary entries, up to April 1994, were published in Zagreb in their original language.**

Elma's text displayed the same extraordinary catalytic quality on this side of the Atlantic. The work precipitated the formation in Toronto of the Sarajevo Collective, a group of "hyphenated Canadians" representing various Yugoslav nationalities, who have produced a one-woman play about Elma based on her diaries and letters. And, of course, there is this book.

What accounts for the power of her writing? In the first place, there is the forcefulness and immediacy of her voice. She is a passionate, strong-minded woman, who invites engagement rather than sentimentality. And she has a novelist's eye and ear. Like any good writer, she speaks out of her truth. Her story is not a catalogue of horrors – the worst atrocities of ethnic cleansing are only alluded to, for they have not become part of the

---

*One of the *mahalas* – residential quarters, or neighbourhoods – of Sarajevo.

**Spoken by Serbs, Croats, Muslims, as well as local Jews, Gypsies, etc., alike, with regional variants and dialects governed by geographical rather than ethnic boundaries, and variously called Serbo-Croatian, Croato-Serbian, Serbian, Croatian, and now, Bosnian. There are subtle lexical and phonetic differences between the language of Elma's manuscript, the "Croaticized" version published in Zagreb, and the South Serbian variant I speak, but they are essentially the same language. As a Croatian woman I once spoke with put it, "All we South Slavs can understand one another; we just don't want to."

experience of the citizens of "free" Sarajevo, though always hovering at the edge of their collective consciousness is the possibility that they one day could. The framework of her narrative is daily life: the mundane and familiar details of housekeeping, work, and social relations, transposed onto the bizarre background of war. Her outlook is secular, middle-class, urban, Western. She is a fan of Monty Python and Douglas Adams's *Hitchhiker's Guide to the Galaxy*. The categories through which she interprets her experience are immediately recognizable: bombed-out ruins suggest to her a planetary landscape in deep space; her own life often seems as surreal to her as it does to us, as though she has found herself in an old black-and-white war movie, a B film she is nevertheless determined to sit through to the end. Her life has been reduced, in material terms, to bare essentials and less, but her curiosity, compassion, and *appetite* for experience remain undiminished.

More disconcerting for Western readers is the recognition that her world, rendered so deliberately and thoroughly alien by the abstractions and obfuscations of UNspeak, is actually very close to ours, too close for comfort. As she reminds us repeatedly, at first in a tone of "God forbid," then increasingly of "good on you!": the Sarajevo show of '92 is on the road, coming soon to a theatre near you. Her world of Western culture did not insulate her from the barbarians at the gates with their pseudo-medieval rhetoric of blood and glory and crusades against the infidel. Neither, we are left to conclude, will ours. Perhaps that is why the West has chosen to throw up its hands at those impossible South Slavs with their innate bloodlust and incomprehensible feuds. To affirm solidarity would be to admit vulnerability and to acknowledge the true character of the conflict. The siege of Sarajevo and of the other "safe havens" (urban islands of Bosnian civilians in the sea of Serbian expansion) is an attack upon the city, upon the very fabric of urbane, civilized existence. Elma says this explicitly, and she is not the only one.

In the final analysis, all the international resolutions and condemnations, the polemic and counter-polemic (in which both Elma and I love to indulge), all the hard facts and reliable estimates, when confronted with the reality of human suffering and death, sound at best irrelevant, and at worst, insane. Human caring is the only thing that continues to make sense.

As for Elma and her family, where are they now? Elma's sister, Ilona, has left Sarajevo and moved to Tasmania. Her father continues to work as a physician in a Sarajevo clinic; her mother has retired from her career of teaching German and English. Her grandmother is still alive at ninety, but has unfortunately gone quite senile. Elma herself decided to pass up an opportunity to move to Israel. She is currently working as a secretary for Marie Stopes International, a UN aid organization. She married Pavle Kaunitz in September, 1994. On July 21, 1995, amid some of the worst bombardment and deprivation the city has experienced thus far, a daughter, Hana, was born to them. They moved back in to her parents' apartment on Alifakovac. The past few months have brought something which resembles peace, or at least an end to war (though, as Elma says, "this end is not a real end") but not security.

Nada Conić

Editor's Note

Great care was taken to present Elma Softić's letters and diaries in their entirety. However, some material has been omitted from the final text. The decision to omit material was based solely on its repetitive or very personal nature, and on no other considerations. Some of those omissions are indicated by [...].

8 April 1992

In Bosnia-Herzegovina. Chaos.

The whole city is organizing. In the buildings and passageways patrols are being organized. Basements are being fixed up.

The radio and TV are reporting that Sarajevo is swarming with snipers.

People are besieging the bus depot and the airport. They're leaving Sarajevo. Planes are taking off for Belgrade. People are fleeing in panic. As far as possible from this city, from Bosnia, from Yugoslavia....

A police curfew from 10 p.m. to 6 a.m. – an excellent cover for the gangs that are looting the shops. The city has been handed over to criminals.

THE NEW YORK TIMES, APRIL 8, 1992

U.S. Recognizes 3 Yugoslav Republics as Independent

By DAVID BINDER
WASHINGTON, April 7 — The Uni-   pressing for United States recognition of Croatia and Slovenia, the Adminis-tration took pains to explain its ratio-

10 April 1992

As of this morning the Work Obligation Law *[making work attendance compulsory and defining hours of operation for strategic and other industries]* is in effect. Dad went to work. The streetcars have been in operation since six o'clock in the morning. I went out. The stores were closed. Bread is being sold from bakery trucks at specified locations. Milk too, but there is much less of it – in total, 16,000 litres for a city of 500,000 inhabitants. There's no chance we'll get any.

Ilona and I are sleeping in sleeping bags in the safest corner of the apartment, if there is such a thing as a safe place in this apartment. I used to like the fact that it's so full of light, with huge windows. Now I wish I lived in a stone tower, and in the basement at that, twelve metres underground.

13 April 1992

TV Belgrade is talking rubbish, like this: in the Old City people are blowing up their own property themselves in order to provide a cover for their persecution of the Serbs.

And in other cities in Bosnia-Herzegovina, chaos: Višegrad, Foča, Kupres, Bosanski Brod, Mostar, Čapljina.

Refugees are streaming in all directions.

15 April 1992

A meeting at school. Mom and I went by taxi. We submitted marks for the trimester. Where there was no mark, I carried over the final mark from the midterm; where there was a 1 *[failing mark: 1, 2, 3, 4, 5 = E, D, C, B, A]*, I added a mark *[i.e., for non-existent term work]* and put down a 2 (luckily, I didn't like to hand out ones).

I submitted marks right away for the end of the year as well – there's no chance of the students returning to school before the end of the academic year. This is not going to come to an end so soon. It's only just begun, I fear. The rest of the teachers are more optimistic: they're submitting marks only for this trimester.

21 April 1992

At 4:55 this morning the bombardment of Sarajevo began. There was shelling across the entire city, but mostly in the old part. The Electric Company building was bombarded, GRAS *[Gradski Autobusni Saobraćaj = city transit]* once again. It went on till after 8 a.m.

All day long you could hear bursts of machine-gun fire, single shots, and distant explosions.

Around 5:30 p.m. the bombardment started up again. That was the worst afternoon and the worst night so far. From half past five, when it

11

started, it didn't stop until after two in the morning. It was terrifying listening to the approach of the explosions – every bomb that fell was nearer than the last. That's unendurable – you're just waiting to be blown to pieces. You breathe a sigh of relief when you hear one fall farther away than the preceding one – it's receding. And it doesn't let up. There were several times when I was certain that the bomb had landed on the pavement in front of our building. It was horrific. The five of us squeezed into that corner by the main door – crammed into two square metres – and waited for it to pass.

When the first shell landed in our immediate vicinity, I got diarrhea. Ilona is frightened. So is Dad. You can read Mom's terror and despair on her face. My terror manifests itself in irritability. I curse, I shout, everything annoys me.

Now, at 3:35 a.m., instead of sleeping (things have quieted down), I'm writing. I wish I could describe to you the terror and anxiety I felt. All I know is that I was afraid, that I had diarrhea, and that I was covered in a cold sweat. Shudders of horror went through me, my throat was constantly constricted, and I thought that I wouldn't be able to stand it, that I would simply die.

22 April 1992

The worst night (so far – it can certainly get even worse, assuming that we all stay alive) is now over. This morning the shelling started around six, but it wasn't nearby.

I went out to buy bread. Full of fear of what I might find, because I was convinced that in the course of the night at least half of the neighbourhood had ceased to exist. I was sure that Tito Street from the department store to the Eternal Flame* was in ruins. I was totally confused when I saw that all the buildings were still standing in place, and I was appalled by the atmosphere of desolation that overwhelmed me the moment I stepped into Tito Street. The sidewalks and roadway were filled with glass

---

*A flame which burns at a monument to the dead of World War II.

and plaster dust, the windows and their displays were shattered. Except for two or three people who had started to clean up the enormous quantity of glass, there was nobody around. I was gripped by fear and I almost began to cry. One single question spun round in my head: What would I have done if I had actually come across honest-to-goodness ruins?

I didn't find bread even though I went all the way to Baščaršija**. On my way back I ran into more and more people. The streets were filling up. I was already at the corner by the department store when a man passed me with an armful of round loaves. I asked him where he'd got them and he told me – in one of the two small bakeries in the Bazaar *[čaršija]*. So back I go: in front of the bakery, a crowd; they've run out of bread, and people are waiting for the next batch. I stand and wait, too. I eavesdrop. People are talking about what they've been through the previous night, cursing. [...] I managed to buy two loaves of bread.

By now the streets are relatively full. It's a gorgeous day, and people are walking and looking around. They all have a fearful air about them, despite the fact – and this really caught my eye – that they're generally well dressed, the women are wearing make-up, no one is in a hurry. Small groups are forming, and from the fragments of conversation floating past me I perceive everyone is talking about the war which is here for real. Not a single store is open.

Up in Alifakovac, a shell landed on the roof of Nedžad's house. All our outer windows on the street side were broken as well as almost all the interior ones. The walls have been pockmarked by shrapnel, both on the outside and in the rooms. One piece of shrapnel whizzed through a double-glazed window, then through the brass body of the chandelier, and slammed into the opposite wall. The porcelain drops *[i.e. hanging decorations: she calls them "little bowls"]* on the chandelier remained intact. All together, twelve windowpanes were broken.

I was in school – looking from the streetcar stop, through the city, you can see the sky above Grbavica *[the Serb-held suburb of Sarajevo]*.

**The name of the central market square, dating from the Ottoman period. A čaršija is a bazaar, a covered market.

Clashes on Ilidža and Sokolović-kolonija. All morning the radio has been broadcasting appeals to allow fire engines through to extinguish the blaze near the Medical Institute, which has sixty bedridden patients.

The Institute has caught fire. It's now 3:30 p.m. The firefighters still can't get through.

In Ilidža, many dead and wounded.

At 6:30 p.m., the shelling has begun again. The shells are not landing far away, and they're getting closer and closer.

24 April 1992

Europe is dithering – she's looking for some kind of solution, offering advice; now and then some diplomat or other includes Sarajevo in his holiday itinerary. Next thing you know someone flies into Sarajevo, and then some ceasefire agreement is signed. As long as the foreign tourists are here, there's no shelling. Zoom, they're gone, and the shells start raining down. The ceasefire agreement is a signal to everyone to head for the basement five minutes before it comes into effect – every ceasefire begins with a bombardment.

THE WASHINGTON POST, APRIL 28, 1992

Bosnia's Problems Mount Under Serbian Siege

BOSNIA, From A1 — ternal "customs posts" are severely hampering UNHCR's $31 million — what he envisions for the capital, he has cited the examples of Berlin,

29 April 1992

Last night we were in the shelter again. Only in a chilly, smelly, dark basement, three metres underground, do I feel human. Absurd – only in the basement do I become a free and strong being. Because in the basement there is no fear.

I hate fear. I have not got used to it. I have never been a fearful person and I did not have an accurate conception of what fear is. Fear is loathsome.

14

It is paralysis, death. I cannot stand the terror that overwhelms me while I'm waiting for a bomb to go off, hoping that we will once again be spared.

That's why, as soon as we see that a nasty bout of shelling is on the way, Ilona and I are the first to take our backpacks and head for safety, while the others follow. And when I find myself in that windowless hole, full of coal dust, humidity, and stench, there comes over me a delicious sense of relief, and I can't conceal my pleasure at being here where I am, where I no longer have to be afraid.

I don't think I'm afraid of death. I'm afraid of fear. I wonder, if this goes on long enough, maybe I'll even get used to it. They say people get used to anything.

The bombardment lasted until after one. Shells were falling over the entire city. A lot of them landed in our immediate vicinity. It looks as though the CSB *[Centar službene bezbjednosti – Department of Social Services, a kind of welfare office]* was targeted yet again.

There was also gunfire around the house. I thought I heard someone running and shooting – maybe they were after some sniper again.

There's talk that the city is full of idiots who are shooting at passers-by indiscriminately: men, women, children, it's all the same to them. And why should it matter to them, when they're allegedly getting 500 Deutschmarks per hit? They say that there are many natives of Sarajevo among these hired guns, people who were born and educated, made friends, and started families here. And apparently there are some from every ethnic group. In point of fact, they all belong to the same nation: the nation of paid killers.

There are, however, a greater number of "newcomers" among these killers. The type who at some point forced their way down from their mountain caves and shambled into the city. The asphalt gave them blisters, the traf-·fic made their heads spin, the elevators terrified them, the apartment buildings and high-rises made them claustrophobic, the books proved their intellectual inferiority, and now they have their revenge! They kill and destroy. Perhaps the doctor of philosophy, the professor at the University of Sarajevo, supposedly an expert in German classical idealism, a man who might have been my mentor, has interpreted Rousseau in a manner incomprehensible

15

for a civilized being. He has understood the return to nature quite literally: that is, he is quite literally destroying the city (remember, Professor, the city – is civilization). *[Nikola Koljević, Karadžić's deputy, was a professor of world literature and a prominent Shakespeare scholar at the University of Sarajevo.]* The shelling and shooting notwithstanding, I slept through the greater part of the night. On a trunk in the basement. Truly, people get used to anything.

THE NEW YORK TIMES, MAY 1, 1992

Their Image Poisoned, The Serbs Voice Dismay

By JOHN F. BURNS
Special to The New York Times

BELGRADE, Yugoslavia, April 30 | From Kosovo to Jasenovac, the — Over an embassy dinner here the | World War II death camp in Croatia

2 May 1992

Here we are in the basement. It's now 4:20 p.m. At 1:30 p.m. a ghastly bombardment began. See, I got ready to do some writing, but now I can't.

THE NEW YORK TIMES, MAY 3, 1992

Sarajevo's Center Erupts in War, Weakening Yugoslav Truce Effort

By JOHN F. BURNS
Special to The New York Times

BELGRADE, Yugoslavia, May 2 — | Bosnia and Herzegovina recognition as A fierce battle involving tanks, ma- | a state independent from Yugoslavia chine guns and rocket-propelled gre- | early last month, continuing the dis-

3 May 1992

It's now 9:30 a.m. [...] According to the radio reports, the city centre is badly damaged. The Post Office building is on fire, and from our window we can see billows of black smoke. The Trade Union building is burning. There's no power. Our phone line is dead. There are no telephone, telegraph, or fax communications. We are completely cut off, not only from the outside world, but also from the rest of the city.

We listen constantly to the news. We're the only ones in our section of the building with a transistor radio. There's no telling how long we'll be without electricity and how long our batteries will last.

This morning, also, you can hear infrequent and relatively distant explosions. Nevertheless, the atmosphere in the building is dreadfully tense, and the calm that comes in from the street through the open window is no less threatening. On the contrary. Everyone around me is waiting for something to happen. The day would be clear and sunny if it weren't clouded over by the smoke and soot from the fires.

None of us has gone outside, and all of us are ready to go to the basement, so we don't get caught as we did yesterday, when at the moment that the bombs started falling we were all in light summer clothing. Still, if it continues to be peaceful, I will go outside to see what happened yesterday and last night.

The radio is announcing that there are dead and injured lying in the streets, and appeals are constantly being made to allow ambulances through and not to shoot at them.

The night before last – the night of the first and second of May – fierce battles were raging in the lower part of the city, and shells were falling on the Old City as well. Downtown was relatively quiet.

In spite of the shooting and distant explosions that could be heard all morning, we behaved as if nothing out of the ordinary was happening. As a matter of fact, nothing out of the ordinary *was* happening – we've been listening to explosions for a month now, now nearer, now farther away. All the windows in the apartment were open, we were half-naked, in short sleeves, without socks, Grandma's things for the basement were scattered in a million directions – to be aired out. (Never, but never does she keep all her basement stuff together, in one place, and every time, she goes through the whole apartment searching for everything she needs and collecting it, and, naturally, she always leaves something behind, partly because she forgets and partly because she stubbornly insists that she won't need it.) Mom was in the kitchen, Ilona was in Grandpa's room, I was in the dining room, and Grandma and Dad were on the balcony (on the one facing Radičević Street) – drinking coffee. Naturally, this was at Grandma's insistence because, by God, it was such a lovely day, and peaceful (she doesn't hear it even when bombs hit the department store, let alone when it starts "shivering" in Bistrik) and so she wants to "have a coffee on the balcony," and what's the matter with us that nobody wants to keep her company, she's lonelier now with five of us in the house than she was when she lived alone. It was no use trying to explain to her that the radio is always broadcasting warnings to citizens not to linger in front of windows or on balconies or in open spaces in general. And our balcony opens wide onto Mt. Trebević.

Suddenly, very close, there was the sound of a shot being fired and a bullet whistling past. Even I heard it in the dining room. And a dull thud. I heard Dad shoving a chair aside and shouting to Grandma to get down. I rushed into the bedroom and saw Dad on the floor below the balcony window; Grandma began to fuss nervously around the coffee cups. Finally she came in. I hurried back into the dining room and called to Mom to get out of the kitchen. Dad said that after the shot was fired he heard the bullet hit the front of the building, and this morning we found the place where it struck. We didn't find the bullet. Well, someone was not pleased that the two of them were so impudently enjoying a midday coffee on a Sunday.

That was when the shooting started in earnest, here, right under the window. […] And after that, the explosions. And they were getting louder and closer all the time. The five of us cowered in that famous corner by the main door.

Zora called some twenty seconds before the first terrifying explosion. Dad answered the phone. She asked whether by any chance I had gone off *[to Alifakovac]* because she wanted to warn me, whether I was here or up there, to stay put at all costs, because a neighbour of hers who had just come from downtown had told her that the JNA *[Federal Army]* Officers' Club was under attack. At that a bomb burst, the first in a series of terrifying explosions. Dad ended the conversation and huddled in his place in

18

the corner. It was 1:20 p.m. Those were the most powerful and closest explosions yet, and probably also the largest calibre of shells. Through the open windows we heard the breaking and crashing of glass. That was an unbelievable experience. Terrifying, but new, and therefore exciting. That may sound perverse, but that's how it was. I know that in the moment the glass was shattering, I experienced the same feeling I did on the morning of the terrible earthquake in Montenegro. On that occasion, as I was standing in my pyjamas, scarcely awake, in the doorway, I felt the walls trembling beneath my palms, which I was pressing against the door frame, and I felt a twisting and a peculiar, thrilling shudder of fear in my stomach. My guts were in knots, I was horribly afraid, but my one and only thought was that I had never experienced anything like this and that I didn't want it to stop. And for the entire rest of the day after the earthquake, regardless of my horrible fear and regardless of the dreadful news reports that were reaching us from Montenegro, I was conscious only of this single thought: I wanted to experience that again. It was like that yesterday as well – I was in spasms and shaking and sweating all over and I was hideously cold, my heart was bouncing between my navel and my throat and it felt as though I was about to explode, but that strange excitement compelled me to prolong each sensation in my own body and – I simply didn't want it to end.

That moment, the moment of that first explosion, was horribly long, and now I can't understand how it was possible for me to think so many thoughts, to see and feel so many things in that one single instant, in the short time required for one explosion. In that moment I saw, actually saw, even though my head was between my knees and even though there was no way I could see anything because I was facing the wall, nevertheless, I *saw* the windowpanes on the building across the street quite simply, as if torn off, all at the same moment as though they were connected, with the sunlight still flashing inside them, come tumbling down.

After two terrifyingly close hits we smelled the odour of gunpowder and heard, in the pause between the explosions, the thud of masonry, presumably chunks broken off the façades of buildings somewhere, and the rustling of leaves from the falling branches of the birch tree in front of our house.

19

The explosions became so powerful and came so near (in fact I couldn't grasp how a mortar shell could fall closer than any had previously without killing us, and yet the explosions were getting ever louder) that we flipped over the dining-room table to see if we couldn't protect ourselves (yeah, right) even a little bit from possible shrapnel. How little human beings need! How little they need to feel safer! I suspect I would feel better even behind a tulle curtain than I would without one. (Actually, Emir told me how their lace curtain managed to trap all kinds of tiny pieces of shrapnel.)

Meanwhile, in our home, to bring the comedy to a climax, the usual "barricades," namely, pillows and blankets in the windows, dressers against glass doors and similar defensive measures that were supposed to protect us against broken glass, were not in position, because, as I said already, it was a lovely day and we had taken the whole place apart to air it out.

Around 2 or 2:15 a.m. we heard the Mrgans go down to the basement. They knocked on our door. The building continued to shake from the blasts. We didn't want to go downstairs while the bombs were falling, not down that horrible staircase open towards the back yard, in which a number of shells had landed in the last hour – three or four – and whose window frames (the windows are huge, from floor to ceiling) still held fragments of thick, reinforced glass.

At the first break in the shelling, Ilona and I grabbed our backpacks (in them we always keep everything we need for the basement – from clothing and food to items like candles, soap, etc.) and rushed down the stairs. Not that the break was any kind of a break, because the pounding started up again. We had the impression that some part of the building was struck while we were still on the stairs. Mom had to get all dressed, because she was wearing a summer dress, and the things for the basement were hanging out on the balcony – they were airing out, of course. Dad and Grandma were the last to come down because, as I've said, Grandma's stuff is always in a thousand places, and this time she was so frightened that she just couldn't get it together.

It was 2:30 a.m. when the five of us finally gathered in the basement. All the other tenants were already there. Almost all: Ilija Duka, who is unwell and rather overweight, and Rade Vujičić, also a sick man, never used to come down, and they didn't then, either. Their wives told us that both of them took their usual dose of tranquillizers and that they were sitting in the front room of the Vujičićs' apartment on the third floor. Later on they did come down, too, probably when their tranquillizers, the most sought-after medicine in Sarajevo this last month, stopped working.

The pounding went on all day. Bombardment of the intensity I have tried to describe was, I think, at first confined to downtown and then spread to all parts of the city. The power went out about two, and on the news we heard that the telephones had stopped working. It looks as though this happened about five in the afternoon. It was announced that 45,000 telephones in the city had gone dead.

Somewhere around seven in the evening a plane carrying *[Bosnian president Alija]* Izetbegović and Zlatko Lagumdžija*. Both of them had been at the negotiations in Lisbon. Anyhow, the result of these consultations, negotiations, delegations, and whatever, as far as I have been able to grasp it with my modest intelligence, is approximately this. *[Portuguese foreign minister]* Cutilheiro said: Clean up your mess, stop the "conflict" (you hear that – conflict!), and then we'll carve up Bosnia ethnically and territorially!

Well, when Alija flew in, the army came (I'm talking about our dear "people's" one – I feel sorry for any people with such a "people's army" that defends it by dumping tons of bombs on it) and zap! they seized the abovementioned individual, who is also, by the way, the state president! To ensure his security. They arrested the president for his own safety. Bravo, people's army!

And then it started: the negotiations, the agreements, the ultimatums, the threats, the requests. And all that hullabaloo was transmitted into the ether, so everyone could hear the hysteria that seized hold of all the people who suddenly found themselves in the role of "key players." The phone lines were severed so that neither the Presidency nor the military command

*Vice-president of the ruling SDA, the Party of Democratic Action.

21

nor UNPROFOR could establish a direct line of communication; instead, everything went via the RTV* station. That's not such a bad thing. On the contrary, it's a good thing. If anyone had any illusions about all this bullshit, now they're dead and buried. At least they should be for sane people.

The conditions of the Republic of Bosnia-Herzegovina were as follows:

1. an immediate ceasefire,
2. the return of Izetbegović,
3. the clearing of a route to Lukavica for the army so that the tanks and armoured personnel carriers could return whence they came.**

And what were tanks and armoured personnel carriers doing in the city in the first place? On whom were tanks and armoured personnel carriers firing yesterday in the city? On Green Berets? I don't have a green beret. I bet the army was really scared shitless when their tanks were fired upon in the streets of Sarajevo by the "Green Berets." It's not as if I or the vast majority of people know exactly who or what they are. But we know for sure that they don't have tanks. Not in Radičević Street. A tank isn't a TV remote that you can shove in your pocket.

The army, naturally, objected to the order of these conditions. Their terms were as follows:

1. an immediate ceasefire,
2. clearance to collect and transport the dead and injured,
3. the release of Izetbegović.

Now it's 1:45 p.m., and I'll stop here, for the moment.

It's midnight. Today we made two trips to the basement. Both times on account of the nervous tension that hasn't left us since yesterday, despite the fact that downtown, at least here around us, it was quiet. […] We were thrown into a panic by a mortar shell that whistled by over the building. It's an appalling sound. We didn't hear it explode, but we went downstairs just in case.

*Radiotelevizija = the state broadcasting corporation.
**Obviously, Izetbegović was being used by the army as a hostage to guarantee them safe passage out of Sarajevo.

There were alarming reports from the CSB. Mirsad Tokača was warning of a night of heavy bombardment. It seems to me that he said at least a million times that today's quiet was only an illusion and the calm before the storm.

I did go around Sarajevo. Actually, I ran down a few streets. I recall nothing except my own horror. As we were coming back up from the basement, I think it was around 4:30, I ran outside. I wanted to see what happened yesterday, no matter what. Radičević Street was deserted. I didn't have the courage to go down Tito Street and so I went down JNA Street. The Street of the Yugoslav National Army. Lord! Lord, what are you doing to us? The tanks of that very army were pounding that very street and its inhabitants. I was running in earnest – partly because I had slipped out secretly and I didn't want my family to get worried, partly out of fear that it might start all over again and that I might be caught in an empty street without any chance of returning home or of taking cover somewhere. It seems to me that by the Obala *[riverbank; the street, whose full name is Obala Vojvode Stepe Stepanovića, follows the north bank of the Miljacka River]* by Poštanski Most *[Post Office Bridge]*, there was a body lying in the street. If it was, then that was the second corpse I had seen in my life, but I'm not sure. I didn't go any closer. Perhaps it was just an ordinary rag. I ran on. By Drvenija there really were corpses on the ground. I didn't stop, I didn't slow down.

4 May 1992

There was a powerful blast just now, relatively nearby. Anxiety has crept up from my stomach to my throat, and my heart is pounding. I've lost my concentration, I can't write. And I'm afraid. My throat feels as though I have tonsillitis. I know that the easiest thing for me to do now would be to take cover by the front door and either to huddle and wait, or else to walk in a circle six paces in circumference and, once again, to wait. And once again with a huge pit of anxiety in my stomach, both sweating and

23

freezing at the same time, with attacks of an ever greater fear which comes flooding over me, squeezing my chest and my heart and my throat, with a dreadful anticipation which makes me feel as though my heart will burst from the tension and that at last everything will return to its proper place. Every organ which is slowly rising up to just under my palate in terror will descend to its proper place and I will relax, once and for all.

I'm afraid here in Grandpa's room, I'll be afraid by the front door, too, therefore it makes no difference, except that sitting here is, even so, more dangerous.

And here I go again, chattering needlessly. The fear from that explosion is not letting up at all, and I feel better this way – as long as I write I feel much better – but now I can't even write any longer.

Ten hours later: [...] The blasts started again, powerful and nearby. Then two airplanes flew overhead, and for the first time, the air raid siren went off. The news is horrific: the aircraft fired rockets on Zlatište, the UNIS building, and the TV transmitter on Hum. And worse yet, chemical warfare: the planes released two components, some yellow substance and a green one, whose combination is toxic.

5 May 1992

Today it was confirmed that what the airplanes were spraying yesterday was some sort of mild irritant.

All day yesterday the director of Pokop *[funeral services]* was broadcasting public appeals over the radio to allow hearses to pass through and not to shoot at cemetery workers attempting to bury the dead, of whom there are, apparently, a great many. In Lenin Street at number 14 and at another higher number, corpses are being piled up; and it's like that in other parts of the city as well. Pokop is in the news again today: the director announced that the company is suspending all operations until further notice, as there have been casualties among the workers, who were shot while trying to inter the corpses.

That means: contagious diseases are on their way.

Blood, tears, screams, death – that is Sarajevo. Buildings in ruins: shattered, charred, looted. That is Sarajevo.

Last night Baščaršija was on fire yet one more time in its long history. The firefighters were desperately calling on the citizenry to come to their aid, for there were so many fires in the city they couldn't keep up, and besides, they're exhausted, after days of extinguishing fires in all parts of the city. The citizens of Sarajevo, naturally, responded.

The Bey's mosque has been hit, Ali-pasha mosque has been damaged, Kujundžiluk and Bravadžiluk have also suffered. Zlatarska *[Goldsmiths']* Street has been demolished and robbed – the overall conclusion: the maniacs who bombarded it were not the ones who pillaged it. In the bomb shelter someone said: "From above Vasko – from below Hasko." *[Vasko = Vasilj, a typically Serbian name; Hasko = Hasim, which is Muslim.]* The upper storey of the lovely house by the cathedral, the one with the School of Electrical Engineering on the ground floor, burned down; Tito Street is covered in broken glass; in Zema *[department store]* a huge crater – a quarter of the wall on the second floor is missing. Last night the Parliament building was also on fire.

On Hum hill eighteen Muslims were massacred. [...] In Grbavica, in Lenin Street, the Chetniks drove Muslims out of their homes and used them as a human shield. What's happened to Sudo?* They were doing the same thing in Vogošća.

In Dobrinja even today, since the ceasefire took effect at 10:30 a.m., they've been forcing Muslim men out of their homes and killing them. The report hasn't been confirmed (it must be confirmed by at least three sources), but it's certain that they're taking them away. They drive the women and children out of their homes and steal everything they can get their hands on.

Today, in Dobrinja IV, some "refined" citizens are looting shops and carrying off everything – from needles to washing machines.

---

*Her great-uncle, i.e., her mother's father's brother, Sudo Gavrankapetanović, a prominent Muslim lawyer.

25

Marat *[sic – his name is actually Marrack]* Goulding is in Sarajevo. (He's the previous version of Vance, the representative of Boutros Boutros-Ghali.) He took off from Beograd airport in a military helicopter and landed in – Pale. There he was held for six hours. The Yank declared that this was entirely unnecessary and that he had lost precious time, and that he would report this to the United Nations. [...] They took him hostage, held him for six hours, and he's going on about his lost time. Where was he off to in such a hurry – to a round of golf? All this fuss over the fact that Mr. Goulding lost precious time. What is the penalty for kidnapping in the U.S.?

When the aforementioned official finally schlepped into Sarajevo, his welcome salute was a bomb that exploded in the immediate vicinity of the PTT, and his farewell salute was similar: just as he was standing in the doorway, a bomb landed in the parking lot in front of the building.

I'm not sure I know why the fellow in question came at all, but as far as I can figure out, it was probably to size up the situation (it's about the millionth time that foreign tourists have come to get a look at this game preserve up close – all that's missing is guns so they can start taking shots at us, too). For the time being they're coming just for a photo-safari. How long it will take them to trade their cameras in for big game rifles, I don't know.

The ceasefire has been signed, but the idiots can't tell time. It's now 9:07 p.m., and the so-called ceasefire took effect at 8 p.m. But there's still shooting. It's quite possible that we'll be going back down to the basement.

THE NEW YORK TIMES, MAY 6, 1992

FORCES IN BOSNIA BEGIN TO UNRAVEL

Belgrade Command Gives Up Control, in Effect Handing the Army to the Serbs

By CHUCK SUDETIC
Special to The New York Times

SARAJEVO, Bosnia and Herzegovina, May 5 — Yugoslavia attempted today to ward off possible international

26

It's now 11:55 a.m. The ceasefire was not respected. The periphery of the Old City, the city centre, and Butmir came under bombardment.
There are warnings over the radio that the city is full of snipers.
There are dead and wounded in Dobrinja, but it's impossible to reach them.
The Yanks are rejecting the option of military intervention.

The radio station has organized an SOS phone line so that the citizens of Sarajevo and the rest of Bosnia-Herzegovina can send messages to their families, because there are no other means of communication. I constantly hear: "So-and-so is requesting the son of such-and-such to call him at the following number ...," or "XY of Dobrinja IV wants his parents in the Old City to know that they're all alive and well." Dreadful! How many people lost already? How many of them will never find out what actually happened to their families?

We have no way of making contact with either Raja or Beba or Seka or, especially, Sudo. *[Elma's aunt Raja continued to live in the apartment building on Alifakovac, which Elma's family had abandoned in favour of her grandmother's downtown apartment; about Sudo Gavrankapetanović, her great-uncle, more will be heard.]* We're worried about Sudo. He and his family are on Lenin Street, under heaviest attack by the Chetniks, and yesterday they were forcing Muslims out of their apartments and using them as human shields.

During one month of war, 695 people have been admitted for surgery, mostly serious cases. At the moment there are 309 in the ward; there are shortages of material for bandages, especially surgical gauze, of oxygen and of oil for the generators. These statistics are for the surgical ward of Koševo clinical hospital only.

Mom managed to speak with Sudo, actually with *[his wife]* Ajša. They are very upset. "They" have searched their apartment twice already. "They" were looking for weapons. Ajša speaks of "them" as the "army"; I don't know what she means by that, because there are, it appears, scores of different armies there, all under the command of the SDS *[Srpska Demokratska Stranka: Radovan Karadžić's Serbian Democratic Party, governing party of the breakaway Serb Republic of Bosnia].* For seven days they didn't leave their high-rise. They have no way of getting supplies. People are being taken away. Muslims. Two men were taken from their high-rise. No one knows what's become of them. The Serbian Territorial Defence force called a tenants' meeting at which they informed them that they now belong to the Serbian Republic of Bosnia-Herzegovina. When people said they had no food, they were told that the new regime would take care of that.

Ajša broke off the conversation suddenly. All she said was: "There's someone on the staircase," and the line went dead.

Today I went outside for the first time since the second of May, if I don't count that "dash" down two or three streets on the third of May, which I can hardly recall any more. Tito Street is full of glass and tiny black shrapnel, sand, pieces of brick and tile, broken-off boards. [...] In all of Tito Street, from the department store to the Eternal Flame, only the windowpanes on the Zvijezda pharmacy have remained intact. I wonder how – when all round is dust. [...] I dropped in on Duška – her building was demolished, the left corner completely destroyed, gone. It looks as though it was struck by two of those large mortar shells. I called out to Duška. She answered immediately. No wonder: there's not a single pane of glass, the window frames were torn out. Her orange blinds had been fixed into place with nails with the result that she could neither come to the window nor out on the balcony. I was in a hurry, so I didn't want to come in – the main thing is that the three of them are alive and well.

In Zlatarska Street there's not a single store that has remained intact. The upper two floors of the Privredna Bank by Hotel Europa have been completely burned out – they're black, they couldn't be blacker.

The Post Office building! [...] That gorgeous building! Only the outer walls have survived. Inside it is empty as a seashell. [...] For three days the smoke curled up over that emptiness.

They're bombarding us constantly. [...] Shells are falling in the midst of

28

people walking by, among people waiting in line to buy something. There are always some casualties. People no longer seem to be concerned by the nearness of their own death. They walk along and they die. Like cattle.

Among the razed buildings only shadows will move. The shades of the dead who will come in search of their final minute of life. One by one, until the last person has perished.

1 1 May 1 9 9 2

God created this world. But not out of His goodness; no, it arose from the filthy scourings of the evil cleansed from His own soul. And He, newly pure, went far away from here.

1 2 May 1 9 9 2

Today, all day, the pounding of bombs. We went down to the basement several times. Mom and Dad picked the perfect day to go to Alifakovac. Mom had just crossed Pozorišni Trg *[Theatre Square]* when a bomb landed fifteen metres behind her and killed a woman.

It's a horrifying sound, the whistling that trails after a mortar shell as it flies overhead, but at you least you know it's flying over you. They say it's the one you don't hear that kills you. The one you do hear is already far way at the moment that you register it.

1 4 May 1 9 9 2

A bloody fourteenth of May. The bombardment is horrific. All over the city. […] The dead and wounded wait for hours until someone comes for them. Firefighters are being fired upon. Doctors are being fired upon. Pokop are being fired upon. The Zora chocolate factory is burning, the old tobacco factory in Marijin Dvor is burning, as are the Standard furniture factory, the Social Services building, the Electric Company building, the JAT *[Jugoslovenski Aerotransport – the national airlines]* skyscraper in Vaso Miskin Street, and many homes in all parts of the city.

[...] The radio is announcing the victories of our Territorial Defence force.

1 5 M a y 1 9 9 2

I waited for hours for bread. A mob of people had been standing since early morning by the Eternal Flame waiting for the bread truck. I was suffocating with fear as I stood there waiting for the damn truck, and waiting for a bomb to fall. I couldn't stand it, so I went for a little walk. I went to the market. There were two or three stalls selling nettles and dandelions. In one place two bottles of dishwashing detergent and ten boxes of halvah – and that was all there was to buy at the market.

At nine o'clock I bought two packs of Classic brand cigarettes, at 250 dinars a pack. At eleven o'clock a pack was going for 400 dinars.

I didn't get any bread – it didn't arrive at all.

Today we heard that the Chetniks in Grbavica abducted Miro K. *[Miroslav Kundurović, a prominent Sarajevo gynecologist, a Serb who challenged and criticized Chetniks and Serbian chauvinism.]* There's no news of him. He lives in the same high-rise as Sudo.

1 6 M a y 1 9 9 2

There is no running water. They've bombarded the installations of the pumping station that provides water to the districts of New City, New Sarajevo, and the city centre. Almost the whole city is without water and the greater part of the city is without electricity.

A Fearful Sarajevo Sees
U.N.'s Last Convoys Go

By JOHN F. BURNS
Special to The New York Times
BELGRADE, Yugoslavia, May 17 —
The United Nations today completed

18 May 1992

Today, under the auspices of the Children's Embassy, a convoy of children left Sarajevo for Split. The Children's Embassy called on everyone who has any sort of means of transport (except for bicycles, motorcycles, and horse-drawn vehicles) to participate in the transport of the children. The column was about ten kilometres long. Television cameras filmed the sorrow and grief of the scene. It was dreadful to see the trucks under whose tarpaulins were crammed the children and their tearful mothers. The life of Sarajevo is leaving. The children and their mothers are leaving. Sarajevo is not merely bleeding to death – it is dying of old age. The young men are being killed, the young women are leaving along with their children. The strength, creativity, and intelligence of this city are leaving.

I don't know what to think about this. Keeping the children in Sarajevo means condemning them to possible death or to certain suffering – starvation is doubtless knocking on the doors of the families of Sarajevo. But by escorting them out, we are condemning to death the future of this city, the city that exists now and that its citizens love. What is more important: the life of the individual or of the group? I have always believed that a thriving and promising society is impossible without healthy, courageous, strong, and self-confident individuals. However, is the life of each one of these young people more important than the survival of the community? There was a time when I would have said yes without hesitation, but now I am no longer sure. I don't know how I would behave if I had a child. Would I have the courage to condemn my own child to war and to be in that way the cause of his or her possible death? I don't know.

Where are those children going and when will they return? Will they

31

return at all? Should they return? I myself am only waiting for this war to be over so I can get out of here, on the assumption that I'll be alive and well to see it end. But still, still, my soul aches to see those people leaving. There are some children who are going off with their grandmothers or aunts, with neighbours. Who will take care of them out there? The people here are saying that this cannot go on for long. I'm not sure. Please God, let it stop tomorrow, but I don't believe it will. I don't believe that this war will be over quickly. I fear that it has not yet even begun.

There's one thing I don't understand: bombs are constantly falling, the atmosphere is extremely tense on account of tomorrow's departure of the army from Sarajevo – who had the nerve to organize, under such circumstances, the departure of children?

19 May 1992

Well, this is the day. Today is "D-Day," the deadline for the withdrawal of the *[federal]* army*. This morning planes were flying overhead. The general alert was sounded: a continuous wailing sound lasting thirty seconds (or sixty – I have yet to figure that out). People were literally flying down into the basement in a great panic.

Today one more convoy set out with 5,000 children, and that convoy was halted in Ilidža. The children were taken as hostages! I knew it! I knew that no good could come of this.

20 May 1992

As of today the JNA has been declared an occupying army. About time we straightened that out. I cringe at the thought of the Olympic-style hoopla surrounding the entry of that powerful army with all that powerful weaponry, the army we not only *allowed* to come into Bosnia as it withdrew from Slovenia, but actually *welcomed* with ovations. First you "let in" a vast horde armed to the teeth, then you let them bombard you for a month and a half, and after that you declare them an occupying army. And the people who have denounced them as such are the same ones who, without ado, "let them in."

"There will be no war," Alija *[Izetbegović]* kept reassuring us. For heaven's sake, if he'd only hesitated a little bit before he said "yes" to the army. I remember, while I was watching the TV coverage of the entry of my JNA – for I believed in it, I suppose, right up to the end (that is, until

*The JNA (Yugoslav National Army), the federal army, naturally represented and was located in all areas of the former Yugoslavia. Young males of all nationalities who were eligible for military service served a compulsory eighteen-month term; among the career soldiers, Serbs predominated. When the Serbo-Croat War of 1991 ended with the recognition of the independent state of Croatia, the federal army was allowed by Bosnian president Izetbegović, and with the approval of the United Nations, to "withdraw" from Croatia towards the rump state of Yugoslavia (essentially, the republics of Serbia and Montenegro) through Bosnian territory. As a further gesture of trust and goodwill, Izetbegović allowed the army to confiscate weapons from local territorial defence units, the reservists who were, at the time, the only defenders of BiH. (Dragan Vikić, who appears at Vlado's funeral *[see entry for June 10]*, became a local hero because of his refusal to turn over the weapons of his special police units.) The army, which now belonged to rump Yugoslavia and had no business interfering in Bosnian politics, nevertheless failed to make even a show of neutrality.

Thus, over the night of April 5-6, Bosnian Serb irregulars raised barricades in Sarajevo and attempted to overthrow Izetbegović's government. When the (unarmed) citizenry turned out in the tens of thousands the next day to demonstrate in protest against them, they were fired upon by the JNA. In the following entry *[see May 20]*, Elma recalls her horror at seeing the soldiers remove from their caps the five-pointed red star of Communist Yugoslavia, a sign that they had shifted their allegiance to the "new" Yugoslavia, aggressive and ethnically chauvinist, of Slobodan Milošević.

Throughout the previous winter, JNA units had been digging artillery positions around Sarajevo and other cities, positions from which the Bosnian Serbs would later bombard the civilian population.

Moreover, when Radovan Karadžić's SDS (Serbian Democratic Party) announced a boycott of the sovereignty referendum, JNA planes were used to distribute his leaflets.

It is now generally admitted that the blitzkrieg of eastern Bosnia, during which the Bosnian Serbs occupied over 60% of the Republic of BiH in a matter of weeks, was carried out jointly, after extensive planning, by Bosnian Serb paramilitaries and the JNA, and that the entire campaign was co-ordinated from Belgrade, capital of the republic of Serbia and of the former Yugoslavia. In other words, what Western officials were pleased to call a "civil war" between Muslim, Serb, and Croat "factions" within Bosnia was also, in fact, as Elma at one point describes it, "a classic case of aggression" by a neighbouring state.

Hence Elma's indignation and bitter irony in her subsequent remarks.

33

I saw them remove the red star from their caps), anyhow, I remember that I felt a horrible unease – so much military might in Bosnia could not bode well!

Some people knew, but I didn't believe them. And the reason I didn't believe them was that I was always paying attention to statements, never to arguments. However it was, I was deceived along with hundreds of thousands of others, and now I'm wondering what, if anything, in the last thirty years of my life was the truth.

The convoy with the children is still in Ilidža. Behind this kidnapping is the general Ratko Mladić *[military leader of the Serbian forces in Bosnia]*. [...] Concerning this Mladić, a certain Slovene, a former officer of the JNA and a military theorist, Dr. Geršak, said that with him in the picture, things don't look good for us. As it happens, that we've already seen.

Europe – i.e., CSCE *[Council on Security and Co-operation in Europe]* – insists on producing new declarations concerning Bosnia-Herzegovina. I shit on their declarations. The United Nations have washed their hands of us. The U.S. is all agape – they're saying that Serbia should be pressured with political and economic sanctions. By the time "fraternal" Serbia, along with its "equal" partner Vojvodina and the rest of its equal, compliant, etc. regions that keep it supplied with food, starts to feel the pinch, Bosnia will be totally at peace – all of us will long since be six feet under.

Fuck all of them – the UN and Europe and America – what does the arms embargo imposed on Yugoslavia have to do with us? Why the hell did they rush to recognize us as an independent state when they're still treating us as though we're not? Why don't they lift the fucking embargo from us? The embargo is really going to hurt Serbia – why would they need to *import* weapons when they have the entire *[federal]* army's supply – they could *export* them if they wanted.

In Sarajevo there have been six reported cases of abdominal typhus. I wouldn't mind dying of the plague if I could be sure that it would spread quickly and effectively across the whole planet.

In Dobrinja they're burying the dead in parks. In Mojmilo likewise.

As of 7:30 p.m. the children have neither been allowed to go on from Ilidža nor returned to Sarajevo. They have returned only mothers with infants up to a year old, and not even all of those, because many of them were afraid to be separated from the large group in whose numbers they found some safety – their captors can't possibly be idiotic enough to threaten their lives in any way, when the whole world knows about the kidnapping and ransom. Anyhow, they held the mothers and children in the buses from 6 to 10 p.m., and then they bedded them down in the sports centre on the concrete and wooden benches with no blankets.

The army is still in Sarajevo.

21 May 1992

All those films about the world after the nuclear holocaust are small potatoes compared to what will happen here even without an atomic bomb. The living will start eating the dead, people will kill for a morsel of food. And then, and then this will all spread merrily outwards and set off a world war. (If it hasn't already started – the global powers are playing chess on our backs. Everybody's implicated – they're not feeling any pain yet, but all the symptoms are there.) And one more time all the innate characteristics of the human race will attain their culmination: vileness, evil, perversion, bloodthirstiness, mental derangement, hatred, sadism, all these will once more go marching into the final battle for the conquest of earth's mosaic and the dome of heaven. And opposing the horsemen of the apocalypse will be a sugar-coated bedtime story, pathetic drivel about the power of lovely words, about the everlasting nature of goodness and the advantages of forgiveness, of the necessary and certain victory of the forces of good over the forces of evil. And so, confronting the whole power of wickedness, a pretty lie, no more real than Santa Claus, as long-lasting as a New Year's resolution.

The Presidency has agreed to the ransom: they will have food delivered to the Viktor Bubanj barracks, in exchange for which the monsters will finally release the children. As of 4 p.m. the convoy had not yet set out – they were waiting for UNPROFOR vehicles to provide them safe passage.

The world is expressing its revulsion at the news of the taking hostage of 5,000 mothers and children. And that's all the world is doing.

All in all, the Chetniks just love to hold people to ransom. And why wouldn't they, when it works so brilliantly for them? At the very beginning they put forth an ultimatum: give us back Rajko Kušić (it appears he was *[Nikola]* Koljević's bodyguard), or else we'll bombard Sarajevo. Our side gave back Kušić, and they bombarded Sarajevo. And not just once.

Zetra *[Olympic Sports Hall]* is burning! My gorgeous Zetra! My Zetra whose every inch I know like the back of my hand. The time I spent there was one of the happiest periods of my life.

It was there that I taught children to skate. I trained them to skate the last waltz at the fourteenth winter Olympics, I participated in the closing ceremonies: the Sarajevo Wolf stretched out his hand, to fanfare, to the Calgary Bear. What's the Calgary Bear up to now? He's certainly not trembling in fear of some bomb blowing him to pieces over the Canadian hills. My darling bear, the children who danced around you in '84 are now being killed, and Zetra is burning. Are there among those children being held captive in Ilidža any of the little skaters whom I taught how to keep their balance on the ice and how to fall?

At 5 p.m. the convoy of the Children's Embassy is actually passing through Ilidža. Twenty-two buses and mini-buses and countless passenger vehicles. The children are off to Split.

At the end of this week the Republic of Bosnia-Herzegovina is supposed to be received into the United Nations. Big deal! Just about as big a deal as the UN's determination to help us, and that, I am deeply convinced, is about as effective as a corpse's determination to stop the worms that are swarming over it.

Today Mom was over at M.Ć.'s. *[Full names have been withheld in order to protect the anonymity of those individuals and their families who live in Serb-held territories, and who might therefore be under threat of reprisals were their identity known.]* The man was weeping. B., that maniac, fired seven bullets from a Scorpion *[American-made automatic pistol]* into the kitchen windows while Goran was standing at the stove making coffee. [...] One bullet struck Goran in the head and lodged itself there. He lived another thirty-six hours. He was buried in Bare *["The Marshes," name of the main cemetery in Sarajevo]*. The television station went all out *[evidently, Goran had worked for it]*, and according to M., the funeral took place as it might have in the most peaceful of times – a lot of people showed up who risked becoming casualties themselves of some mortar shell. He left behind three sons and a wife. The oldest child is ten years old. The wife and children had gone to Belgrade as soon as the first shells had fallen on Sarajevo.

Vlado is a real sweetheart. Given that he has a telephone at work, he makes calls to the families of his friends, neighbours, and acquaintances who had the "luck" to be owners of those telephone subscriber lines which fell silent the second of May – until, they say, God knows when.

The radio news reports say that Serbs from Glamoč, Kupres, and Grahovo want to have *[General]* Mladić tried as a war criminal because he forcibly resettled them, razed Kupres, misled or drove them into a fratricidal war, and then fled to Sarajevo. What's this trial, what's this nonsense – they ought to kill him like a rabid dog!

Miralem showed up to tell us that his friend in the Territorial Defence force informed him that a dispatch arrived from the Presidency saying that on the twenty-second of May, in other words, tomorrow, at four o'clock, a general attack on Sarajevo will begin. The agreement among the tenants is to go to the basement at three o'clock. Something is wrong with this picture, if you ask me: what the hell good is an attack that everyone knows about, especially those who are going to be under attack, and why a "dispatch" from the Presidency? But given that I don't know how things operate, especially in a war, maybe it is true. We'll see.

22 May 1992

There was no attack of any kind.

Today Omer told us that a close friend of his had died of starvation. A mutual friend of theirs told him that he had run into the poor fellow, some twenty days after the beginning of the war, and he was half-dead from hunger. He took him home, his wife made him a pita *[meat, vegetables, or cheese between layers of phyllo pastry]* out of what there was in the house, they fed him and even packed him a meal, as much as they could spare, to take with him. After that, the heavy bombardment got underway, and the mutual friend could no longer go visit this man. The man lived alone – no family, a widower, his wife had died two years ago. He died the day before yesterday. They say that he was nothing but skin and bones, and that they didn't find even a crumb of food in his house.

To make the whole thing even more horrifying, that man who died of hunger in the middle of Sarajevo was well off, but to buy any sort of food in Sarajevo these days, you have to be a tycoon, because – there simply is no food. And he had no stock of food. Old people are strange – when we moved in with Grandma, we found in her home half a litre of wine vinegar, a quarter bottle of oil, approximately two kilos of flour, enough butter to spread on three slices of bread, enough cheese for one good-sized sandwich, a handful of pasta, a half-full 500-gram jar of honey, a little tea, approximately half a kilo of sugar; and not one single can, not a pea, not a bit of meat, not a crust of bread; milk – none, cream – none; and as for spices, barely even salt. Not one little bag of soup mix. But nothing. Not a single potato, and as for other fruits and vegetables, let's not mention them. And this in Grandma's kitchen, where in the good old days, there was nothing you couldn't find. And Grandma could afford to indulge herself. And God help you if you tried to bring her something – only a fool would be so reckless as to bring her anything at all, even two bananas, not to mention any basic items, because she doesn't need them, she has what she needs, she doesn't like to have things cluttering up the house, she never eats things like that, and similar bullshit. Well, that bachelor didn't have anything in the house either, he had nowhere to buy anything. Old as he was, he wouldn't have been able to get any bread – not long ago Mom came close to getting suffocated while she was standing in line for bread; she came home completely beside herself and white as a sheet.

4:30 p.m.: Bosnia-Herzegovina was just accepted into the United Nations. RTV is congratulating us. Lucky us. Now the UN will get to work. It will have sittings. It will deliver resolutions. It will sign declarations. It will send protests. It will appeal to reason. It will debate the possibility of sending some new troops. It will decide to impose new sanctions on what now calls itself Yugoslavia.

We'll be lucky if they manage to deliver us some humanitarian aid.

Karadžić & Co. ought to be tried for war crimes, but Europe is working with them to make ethnic maps of Bosnia-Herzegovina. [...] No end to perversions. God, protect me from my friends, from my enemies I'll protect myself!

Well, I really am a jinx. Today Mom managed to get two cartons of milk. By chance. She had gone to throw the garbage into the dumpster and happened upon a truck which was delivering milk to the Territorial Defence force. One of the paramilitaries brought out a crate with twenty litres of milk to distribute to the people. The driver's job was to collect the money, and the people present handed him money and took milk. People gave as much as they had. Mom gave 1,000 dinars, since she had nothing smaller, and she was supposed to get 500 back in change (one litre is 250 dinars), but the man kept the 500 for himself. People were taking what they could get, no one thought to ask about change. Mom was one of the lucky ones! Pašić also paid a thousand, but he didn't manage to grab even one carton of milk. And the poor guy had been collecting money from people – they got some, zip for him.

That was our third litre of milk in forty-eight days, for the five of us! With great impatience I waited all day for a decent time for supper (there's no more of this eating when you want and what you want), so I could make myself some cornflakes with milk. When that solemn moment finally came, in a state of great excitement I opened the refrigerator, carefully took a battered pot that was missing its proper lid and was covered with that ugly blue enamel one which is too big for it, and I turned to put it carefully on the table. The kitchen was dark – naturally, since the "drop" blinds not only do not darken the windows, they light up the dark courtyard as though the sun had suddenly awoken (and a blackout rule is in effect), so we don't even turn on the kitchen light, just the one in the hallway. And what happens? Naturally, klutz that I am, I bang into the edge of the table with the pot, the lid flies off, the milk splashes, and at least 200 mL *[250 mL = 1 cup]* spills out. One whole cupful! It reduced me to tears. So long, cornflakes with milk. I pick up the lid, wash it, cover the pot, and put it back into the refrigerator. What could I do – I didn't have the heart to take another cupful, when I'd wasted one already. Especially when I'd already had some milk first thing in the morning. Luckily for me.

2 6   M a y   1 9 9 2

Our tourism industry is flourishing, that's for sure. Every little while some foreign tourist flies in. And the biggest of our Sarajevo tour guides, Alija Izetbegović, today showed Andrej Kozyrev around Sarajevo. He's the Russian minister of foreign affairs under whose watchful eye another ceasefire was signed which has yielded its first results – the savage bombardment of the Jezero maternity hospital.

The fourth, fifth, and sixth floors of the maternity hospital are on fire. In the building are 130 pregnant women and 70 babies. The babies have already been moved to the basement. The director of the hospital, Dr. Šimić, is weeping. He is asking the Presidency to do something.

THE WASHINGTON POST, MAY 28, 1992

20 Killed, Scores Injured by Mortar Attack on Sarajevo Market

2 7   M a y   1 9 9 2

A massacre in Vaso Miskin Street, in front of Planika, where people were waiting for the bread truck. Three shells landed in the crowd. The bloody bread of Sarajevo. There were about 200 people there. A slaughterhouse. The street running with blood. People lying, mown down. A torn-off foot. Some people are moving, some are screaming for help, others are motionless. The uninjured are running. Some are trying to help – they're carrying away the wounded. You can see shattered legs. One woman's foot is hanging, barely attached, a man being carried by two others has legs that are hanging at a most unnatural angle. A heap of human meat. Blood, body bits. People are arriving in automobiles and trucks, rushing out from the neighbouring homes in their slippers, wringing their hands, weeping, running, looking for the living – the dead can wait.

At 1:35 p.m. they are reading out the names: 124 injured and 12 dead. As of 8 p.m. – 16 dead and 144 wounded.

The maternity hospital has burned down. Up to now, 171,000 children have been born in the hospital. Maybe it was the papa of one of them who set it on fire. Three babies died – from the effects of the bombardment. Because of the power outage the incubators stopped working.

Part of the Marshal Tito barracks is on fire, as are the School of Electrical Engineering and the School of Economics.

The last time I was in the school, I went round the classrooms – the windowpanes shattered, a huge hole in the wall on the third floor, and on one desk the graffito: "Death to fascism, and dammit, to the people, too."

Well, fascism is on the increase, but the people are dying.

28 May 1992

The new figures: 18 dead and over 160 injured.

What we heard during the past ten to fifteen seconds was horrific. A roaring that got louder and louder and the floor shaking as though there were an earthquake. I'm sitting in a basement, four metres underground. Then an appalling explosion which lasted a whole eternity.

The same thing all over again – people are bewildered. Safeta is screaming. We don't know what is happening.

6 June 1992

Vlado has been killed. […] He died last night around eight, while he was listening to "News Journal" in the office, at the time of the heaviest shelling of the downtown. He was killed by an explosion. Heart attack. He, who had been very cautious and responsible, was incautiously and irresponsibly sitting upstairs, in a room overlooking Tito Street, instead of going down to the more-or-less sheltered ground floor. On top of everything, on a night of horrific bombardment. A shell smashed into the wall of the room in which he and one of his co-workers were sitting. Vlado, it appears, was in the direction of the most powerful blast of the explosion. And his heart simply burst. He remained uninjured, not even a scratch.

Vlado was afraid of bombs. [...] I remember that the previous evening, as he was entering the basement because the shells had started to crash sickeningly nearby, he simply remarked, "When I come down to the basement, it's as though I've taken Valium."

And only one evening before his death, he was teaching me how to play rummy and how the cards are ranked. Very patiently and very calmly, he was standing behind me and telling me which card to discard, which to keep, and why.

We saw him for the last time some three or four hours before his death. He had come back from his shift for lunch. He dropped by the basement before going back to work. Ilona, Dragan, and I were cleaning, tidying, rearranging the shelter, while the rest of the tenants were offering us free advice. He halted on the stairs and said, "Good work, good work," raised his hand in a sign of greeting, bending his head forward, calmly, in a slightly comical posture, and with an infinitely charming smile. There, when I think of Vlado, that's how I see him.

[His daughter] Maja is not quite ten, and Marina turned six in February. Their mother told them that Daddy had been wounded, but Maja apparently realized the truth.

7 June 1992

Vlado will be buried tomorrow. Burials have been cancelled because of the bombardment.

Today Vlado was finally buried.

The Graveyard. There were a number of funerals in the Partizan cemetery, where they had stopped burying people at least twenty years ago. Nowadays they call it the Lion cemetery *[because of a statue at the entrance]*. Among others, a certain Vinko is being buried – a member of Vikić's special police units. *[Dragan Vikić, a chief of police, managed to prevent the Serbs from confiscating his service's weapons before the outbreak of the war; his* specijalci, *therefore, became almost the sole armed defenders of Sarajevo.]* Vikić and Divjak* and Doko are in attendance – as are the Chetnik snipers who are shooting from the hills at the assembled people. All at once, a rain of bullets. An appalling hissing sound. In an instant the special force members moved apart and fell to the ground, making a circle around the place they had been standing. Then another spray of bullets. Someone shouted, "Lie down!" and people flung themselves on the ground into the mud. Dad stayed standing, along with maybe two or three others. Then one member of the special forces turned to the people in the cemetery (there was more than one burial in progress) and said, "Go on home, people, we have information that there will be shelling here!" And everyone hurried for cover. The funerals were broken off. Vlado's funeral was already considerably behind schedule.

The Funeral Parlour. We couldn't figure out what was taking them so long, so we went off to the funeral home. There – corpses stacked one on top of another, like logs. You couldn't breathe because of the stench. Nausea and dizziness. They were just putting Vlado into a coffin. An old, worn, wooden coffin. Vlado's hand. The cadaverous, yellow-green hand of something that used to be Vlado. Alongside him they had put his little bag. The one in which he had carried his lunch to work. An ordinary paper

---

*Evidently, Elma is referring to Jovan Divjak, second-in-command of the Bosnian government forces, and, by the way, a Serb.

bag with handles, light brown, with a green and a yellow stripe.

I can't go on like this any longer. The inactivity is killing me. This going off to the basement and coming back to the apartment, going out occasionally to buy bread or to get medicine for Zora's dad. Possibly, going to see the house on Alifakovac.

The Red Cross doesn't need me; they said they would call me if they need people. As for the Civil Defence – when I offered them my services, they stared at me as though I were from another planet. The Civil Defence in this city, it appears, has nothing to do. The headquarters of the Territorial Defence force – doesn't need me. School, of course, is out.

The hospital – I'm considering going to them too to see if I can be of some use there, although I highly doubt it.

In any case, at the first opportunity, I have to find some work. I can't read any more, I can't write. If a bomb doesn't blow me apart first, I'll wilt from boredom, from this vile inactivity.

In the Territorial Defence force there are women fighters as well. I'm considering that, even though I don't know how I would break it to my family that I was going off to the front – they'd have a fit.

The basement – I've had enough of that idiocy. If I've been going down there these last few days, it's more the result of my realization that I have to be alert and disciplined, it's motivated more by the fact that I must do everything in my power to save my life than by fear. I've stopped being afraid the way I was in the beginning. Either I have finally got used to the fear, or else, like so many others, I have started to believe that you cannot live longer than you are fated to, but neither can you die sooner.

To hell with all this nonsense. I've landed in this idiotic war, a war which I will not say is either senseless or needless. Oh, it is full – and how – of meaning, and obviously it was badly needed. Otherwise, it would neither have started nor lasted, look, two full months already. And there are no indications that it will be over in a hurry despite the fact that people continue to hope so. This will last at least another half year – at least for starters. And then there will be a second, third, etc. quarter. Who knows. It's stupid to make plans and predictions.

I have to, I have to find some work.

20 June 1992

As of today a state of war has been declared in Bosnia-Herzegovina. Up till now there has been a state of imminent danger of war. If what has been going on up till now is actually what they say it is, then what's in store for us now? The difference between a state of war and a state of imminent danger of war is this: now a general mobilization has been declared. General mobilization includes the mobilizing of everyone eligible for military service, work obligation round the clock for all essential services, and from 7 a.m. to 7 p.m. for all other businesses.

I continue to think that the world will leave us to kill each other off. They will wait for the situation to settle down – it won't matter to them who has the upper hand, nor will they care whether the Chetniks end up strolling through Sarajevo, the only thing they're concerned about is achieving some kind of *status quo*, a situation in which no one can make any further gains, and then they'll come on the scene as arbitrators, or, to make the whole thing more inane, that is, pathetically inane – as saviours.

26 June 1992

For some days now I have been reflecting on how I have been recording "the wrong things" in this diary. That is to say, everyone is abuzz with the latest information from radio and television reports, but that can also be found in the newspaper, and so I don't need to write about it – I could simply collect newspaper clippings. As a matter of fact, I have started to do that too, and one day I may even organize them properly.

Anyhow, there are lots of "real-life stories" that have been told to me either by the direct participants or by their close friends and relatives, and for which I simply have not found space in the diary. Why is this? Well, I think there are several reasons: one is that it's not a simple thing to describe someone's experience, it's not like merely "transcribing" already processed facts, and despite my need to write, I'm too lazy to get that deeply involved; and the second reason is that I'm never sure how reliable

45

the facts are in these testimonies – people remember only what directly concerns them, the rest passes them by.

On the other hand, even the news I listen to on radio or television and read in the newspaper has undoubtedly been sifted through a multitude of filters, and I don't know from where I got the idea that those kinds of facts are entirely reliable.

The conclusion is, therefore: one should write about what cannot be read in the newspaper, and as far as the truth is concerned – well, one should take a person's word over an institution's, because much more harm is done by institutionalized half-truth than by individual bias.

Yes, well, after such an "intellectual" introduction, how about if I also write down the following three stories.

I .

It's been over a month since A. told us of the torments endured by her cousin who was imprisoned in the Tower *[Kula, the name of a prison which was built in the nineteenth century during the Austro-Hungarian regime, converted into a fancy restaurant after World War II, and now reverted to its original function, thanks to the Chetniks].*

What happened was this: one morning this man appeared at the door of the apartment where S. lives with her [his?] family, here on Radičević Street. They could hardly recognize him: he'd lost weight, aged, grown a beard; he was totally exhausted, filthy, and stinking. The Chetniks had taken him from his home in Dobrinja and locked him up with thirty other people, first in Kula, then they took them off to Pale, then back again to Kula. There thirty people spent ten days in a room that was eight metres by five metres. That's where they slept, lived, were fed a crust of bread and a little cup of indescribable tea, and relieved themselves. They weren't beaten, but they were continually threatened and abused. Every half hour, or at most forty-five minutes, another Chetnik would enter the room and, depending on whether they were lying on the floor, standing, or sitting (as commanded by the previous guard, one of whom was keeping watch over them at all times), he

46

would order them to stand, sit, or lie down. They were forced to lie on their stomach with their arms on their back: "Come on, you Muslim bastards! Lie down, you heard me, right now, or I'll kill you all!" And then, half an hour later, "What's with you people, what are you doing lying down? Sit up!" Then in comes a third one, kicks the nearest man, and barks, "Stand up!" and for the next forty-five minutes, they stand. And that's how it went the whole day long, and on occasion they were tormented like that for thirty hours or more without a break. Curses, threats, abuse, until finally, they loaded them into a truck, drove them to Vrbanja, and ordered them to run across the bridge towards our side. Our soldiers had not been informed that any group of prisoners would be crossing from Grbavica – nothing had been said about any exchange or freeing of prisoners, so it was quite possible, given the murky darkness (it was about 10 p.m.), that they could all be shot dead. The men were afraid to make a run for it, so the Chetniks started to fire shots in their direction, just the thing to give our side the idea that some sort of attack was underway, and in fact, two of the men were wounded – one in the hand, the other in the shoulder. Luckily, one of our fellows realized what was happening and the order was given to hold fire. The men were taken in and brought to the Parliament building, where they spent the night, and the next morning they were released. A.'s relative appeared at the door on Radičević Street early in the morning, unable to speak; he washed and went to bed. He slept eighteen hours, and when he awoke, he stayed only long enough to tell his tale of horror. After that he returned home to Hrasno, more precisely to the apartment in which his family had taken refuge after their expulsion from Dobrinja.

I I.

Two or three weeks ago, our neighbour V.'s brother-in-law, at the insistence of his family, for the first time since the beginning of the war, went down to the basement *[during shelling]*. A mortar shell flew in through the narrow basement window (the shelter was not entirely underground), and the man died from the force of the explosion – he had massive internal

47

hemorrhaging, and very quickly went dark all over. As for external injuries, he had only a few scratches from shrapnel on his legs. His son sustained fairly light injuries to his arm. That was on Koševo Hill.

III.

A sister of that same neighbour V. was taken, along with her son, by the Chetniks from Dobrinja to Kula, and afterwards to Lukavica. In Kula it was horrible. The men were being taken away at night and beaten, and then dragged back, all beaten up, to their cells. They were fed a little bread and a thin tea, and that was their food for the whole day. In Lukavica the army behaved correctly towards them – there was no torture, that is to say, not like at Kula, although on occasion, in the evening, Chetniks might turn up, take someone away, and beat him up – usually it was one of the men. Those who didn't take part in the abuse simply "turned a blind eye" when something like that happened, and – no questions asked. The food was better – they even gave milk to the pregnant and nursing women! Very humane, no doubt about it! On the assumption that we "forget" that they were holding women, children, and expectant mothers in jail!

This war suits every nonentity who sports even the most insignificant official title. Because as long as the war lasts, so will the power of those who are currently in charge. But later, after this hell, if it ever comes to an end, I'm not sure that this tortured and, in the final analysis, deceived nation, or should I say, rather, these deceived human beings, will be in any hurry to elect the same people to the same positions. On the premiss that they will have the power to choose at all.

This war began as a classic case of aggression – they attacked us. The Chetniks. And Serbia. Serbian military units are burning, looting, and killing all over Bosnia. […] But the world is talking more and more about a civil war, and as a matter of fact, all those politicians from the outside world who come here every so often on safari are behaving that way as well – they're waiting for the situation to heat up even further and they're doing everything they can to fan the flames. Europe has bloodied its hands as much as *[General Ratko]* Mladić and the entire SDS combined, with its self-important and stubborn insistence (the mark of a petty spirit) on the cantonization and partition of Bosnia.

My most cherished proverb is the one that says: Protect me, Lord, from my friends; from my enemies I can protect myself. In the last analysis, only a friend can betray you.

In all this bullshit the one thing that really gets me going is this: whenever some ceasefire is signed and Radovan *[Karadžić]* showers us with mortars, rockets, etc., the president, the government ministers, and the news reporters start to go winging to the neighbours – now to Europe, now to the UN, now to the U.S.A. As far as I'm concerned, I'd blithely give away all those neighbours in exchange for a decent quantity of decent weaponry.

And now, back to our menu: the tenants of 15 (formerly 11) Radičević Street, fifth floor, apartment 8, are alternately lunching on peas–macaroni –peas with macaroni; and then again, peas–macaroni–peas with macaroni, and so on to infinity.

27 June 1992

At 5:05 a.m. I was awakened by powerful detonations and terrifying gunfire. In fact, we all woke up and lay in bed, drowsy and sluggish, waiting for the "start" signal for the basement. [...] The first news reports at 6 a.m. informed us that a general attack on Sarajevo was in progress, that artillery was pounding all parts of the city – from the Old City to the airport subdivision, and that infantry was attacking all salients of the front.

However, I don't go down to the basement any more. I'm fed up with it. Given that I had to do something, and I am not quite foolish enough, not yet, to go outside in such "bad weather," I spent the whole morning doing the laundry which had piled up in enormous quantities over the course of these past four weeks when no water made it up to our apartment. At least twenty times I went down to the basement and each time I brought up at least twenty litres of water – today everyone washed everything.

49

The latest news exclusive: François Mitterrand, president of France, flew in to Split this evening around 9 p.m., and tomorrow he will come to Sarajevo! Quite a shock all round. He says that he's doing this to show solidarity with the citizens of Sarajevo. Bully for him – now we feel much, muuuuch better.

I shit on his fairy tale of solidarity. You have to read between the lines, because *[UN Secretary-General]* Boutros-Ghali has declared in the most serious tone that the situation in Bosnia-Herzegovina is steadily deteriorating, and that he will be forced to consider other means of stopping the war in Bosnia-Herzegovina. People are interpreting that to mean military intervention. But that is all a bluff.

Mitterrand's arrival will prolong our agony and will delay the final liberation of Sarajevo and of Bosnia-Herzegovina; that is to say, everyone will devote all their energies to resolving these "conflicts," as they call a war with rivers of blood, by "peaceful means" (only I don't know how they imagine this could be resolved peacefully, when there hasn't been peace for a long time, and this peaceful resolution has cost so many people their lives), and to avoiding intervention, because intervention would undoubtedly jumble the world's accounts.

28 June 1992

Today I'm depressed, sad, and listless. So many people deported, robbed, killed. People like me. People with names similar to mine. People whose only crime is to be disliked by certain other people.

Bah! Nationalism is the most serious form of disturbance of the consciousness of values. The person who is happy and content only when he lives in a ghetto where everyone is the same, where no one is distinguishable in any way from him, that person is definitively lost to culture and civilization, to the world and the future – in a word, to humanity. And I can't help thinking that humanity itself is lost. And has been for a long time.

What's happened to my, *my* Sarajevo? It used to be the most European city in the Balkans and among the "worldliest" in the world – because it accepts differences as a value, and ridicules prejudice and rigidity as so much nonsense. The question is whether this highly lauded "Sarajevo spirit" will be able to survive the death of so many Sarajevans, the stampede of such a herd of invaders, and the systematic annihilation of so many differences, that is, the annihilation of "the unity of diversity."

Now it occurs to me! To what extent am I objective? To what extent is Sarajevo really as I have described it? What if I have been infected with the virus of primitivism of the hometown flag-waving variety?

Goražde is already into the fourth month of a total blockade. A city of 30,000 people is feeding 60,000. According to reports, there is no more food left.

The massacre in Vaso Miskin Street was a month ago yesterday. What was the final tally? Twenty-eight dead, I think. I've forgotten already. Next time it will be 128, and a month afterwards I'll have forgotten that number as well. We've already got used to it. There's that old saying: Death is nearer to you than the collar of your shirt.

6 July 1992

The twelve-year-old girl who was wounded in Dobrinja, while she was sleeping in the same bed as her little cousin whose head was partly blown away by shrapnel, was the daughter of Vesna Šokčević! Dreadful. Dreadful. The children had come up from the shelter to relax and take a nap in a normal bed, since it looked as though the shelling had stopped. The little boy, Filip Šimić, was killed (I remember the eyewitness news report from the man who had run into the room first, a neighbour who was in the apartment at the time and who said that on the pillow, instead of the child's head, was a bloody stain). Vesna's daughter sustained severe head injuries and her chances of recovery, at least given the present conditions and facilities here in Sarajevo, are exceedingly slim. The child needs to be sent abroad for medical treatment, and it looks as though they have got permission to do so from UNPROFOR, or from whichever of those powerful world organizations deals with such matters, and that they will be leaving soon.

Poor Vesna! Poor little girl! All parents and all children who have stayed in this ghastly city are to be pitied. I don't understand, I don't understand, I don't understand.

7 July 1992

Today I was at work. We meet at the offices in Šalom Albaharije Street.

I was happy to see my co-workers, and they were happy to see me. It's a tremendous joy and relief to see them alive. Nevertheless, you hear a lot of terrible stories that leave you shaken.

The Chetniks set up some kind of headquarters in the building where A.S. and her family live. From the moment that those murderers arrived, each new dawn would reveal one or two more emptied apartments. The occupants of the building were not allowed to go out, and they had to keep their front doors open at all times. The Chetniks would enter the homes, ransack them, carry off anything they wanted, make threats. And abduct people. The nights were pierced with the screams of people being tortured. They raped a neighbour, the four of them, before her husband's eyes, then they took him away; the next day she threw herself out the window. (I'm still referring to the victims as "people," it still goes against my grain to attach ethnic labels to them. But I guess it's about time to start. A.S. is a Muslim, the people that they're taking away and torturing are Muslims or, particularly, "disobedient" Serbs. Croats aren't spared either, but it's the Muslims who suffer the worst persecution.)

A.S. was in her apartment in Grbavica with one of her two sons – her husband and other son happened to be on our side on the day when all communications between the two parts of the city were severed. Her son, who is twenty-eight, had a nervous breakdown, and so she decided to get out of that hell at all costs. One of her neighbours, a Serbian woman, obtained for her all the necessary papers as well as the pass she would need to leave Grbavica. They set off, and the neighbour accompanied them partway, until they reached the checkpoint. After that A. had to go on alone with her ill son. On they went; by now it was dark. When they were just about at the bridge and could almost believe they were home free, two tanks loomed into view. They were stopped by the sentries. The youth fell into a fit: he crouched down, started to shake, then just collapsed on the ground. The terrified woman held out her pass, the medical certificate, and a pile of other papers, she started babbling, she doesn't remember any more exactly what – about her son, the hospital, the pass. They were allowed through and told: You can go, but you should know that the terrain you have to cross is mined. So off they went, gingerly, more dead than alive, first on the asphalt, and then across the grass. A. says that their passage seemed to take all night. Finally they came to a bridge (the bridge by the Hotel Bristol). They ought to have made a run for it, but they simply could not muster the strength. At that point shots rang out. Bullets were whistling past them, and run they did. Years and ages passed while they crossed over that bridge. On the far side, our soldiers were waiting. Once again a barricade, once again a suspicious military, with their guns trained on them. The youth, exhausted, collapsed once more, and the woman – luckily only now – lost her self-control. When the sentries saw what a state both of them were in, they waved them on through. A new shock – the buildings in ruins! In Grbavica it was horrible, but there weren't any ruins, and what we on this side were already accustomed to scared them out of their wits. At the School of Economics, a new checkpoint. The young man lost his nerve completely, and when they came to the street that leads to the Brotherhood and Unity Bridge, he started to run towards it – back to Grbavica! By sheer luck, one of the militiamen, an older man, had the presence of mind to shout after him curtly: Stop! and he froze on the spot. That gave them enough time to catch up to him and pull him to safety. They found them a car – actually, they flagged down a truck – shoved them inside and sent them off to the hospital. The youth is still in hospital and is still in very bad shape.

They slaughtered Miro Kundurović after torturing him terribly. At the end they gouged out his eyes and butchered him. Oh, Lord! Oh, Lord! I'm beginning to believe in you and to hate you, and to pray to you. Oh, yes! I'm praying to you more and more often. These horrors can't be accidental, they are the product of some dark and evil power. Could it be yours?

If I end up being convinced that you exist, God, you'll have a terrible adversary, not a powerful one – I am but a tiny creature – but terrible in her implacable rebellion. The revolt of the vanquished. Of the one who becomes all the more determined in his absurd rebellion the more he becomes conscious of his powerlessness. Like Sisyphus.

During the past month in the old-age home in Neđarici *[a district of Sarajevo]* forty old people have died. The home is in a no-man's land and has no communication with the outside world. They have neither food nor medicines.

Mate Boban, that Ustasha, a few days ago announced the existence of the Croat commonwealth of Herceg-Bosna! Bravo! I knew it. Are the Ustasha massacres getting underway now? I hope that the Croats of '92 will have more sense than those of '41. I hope so, but I don't think so. Yes, it's now the Ustashas' turn to go on a rampage. It is, I think, the logical next step. And when will the Muslims start with their massacres? If they haven't already. After all, what's to stop some Mujo*, whose whole family was slaughtered, say, in Foča *[N.B.: Elma's mother narrowly escaped the Chetnik massacre of the Muslims in Foča in '41]*, from charging into some Serbian village and slaughtering all the women, children, and old people he comes across?

As for the lessons of the past, nobody has learned anything. Not the Serbs, not the Croats, not the Muslims. Especially not these last. Serbia has already shown her colours, and Croatia will stick it to Bosnia right to the hilt. As is their custom.

TODAY'S MENU	breakfast:	bread and tea
	lunch:	a soup we call "Wartime Fancy" – water, oil, leftovers of yesterday's soup, a little flour (browned in the oil, naturally) and a little cider vinegar

*Mujo = Mustafa, a nickname for a Bosnian Muslim; *cf.* "Tommy" for an Englishman, "Gerry" for a German.

dinner: bread (today there was no tea for
              dinner since we're totally "dry"
              as far as water goes)

8 July 1992

Around 11 p.m. a terrifying infantry attack was launched, probably against Vrbanja. This is horror. It hasn't been like this for a long time. Bullets are whistling through the courtyard and slamming into the roof of the yellow building in the yard. The bombs are falling very near.

We can't bring ourselves to go into the basement – why take the risk that one of us gets hit on the way down? And it looks as though everyone else is thinking the same thing, because you can't hear the usual ruckus – the slamming of doors and the calling out to the neighbours – of people rushing to the basement. We're sitting in our little corner. We even woke up Grandma. She's turned into a real trooper – she's sitting all prepared and disciplined, waiting to head down to the shelter. I would never have believed that this, too, was possible – Grandma toeing the line. Mind you, the shells are landing very close by, and bullets are whistling from all directions, and it looks as though even she can hear them, and it's obvious that she's afraid.

Bombs are horrific, but it's when I imagine what would happen if the line of defence were breached and if the murderous hordes were to come sweeping down from Vrbanja or Skenderija that I am overwhelmed by terror – with its already familiar and so often described symptoms, the tightened throat and the cold sweat.

If they capture Sarajevo, if they come to Radičević Street, there will be no one or nothing that can save me from violence, and almost certainly, from rape, the fate that awaits everyone whose name isn't Serbian, and especially if their name is Muslim, and I wonder how even the Serbs here would fare, at any rate, the ones who didn't welcome them with a *"pomoz' bog" [traditional Serbian greeting: literally, "God help you"]*.

Madness. Today I heard the personal testimony of a woman from Foča. They're exterminating the Muslims as though they were vermin or pestilence.

They're killing everyone indiscriminately, setting living people on fire, roasting children alive, raping little girls, torturing the men to death.

Vengeance. I'm certain that there must be vengeance – 2,000 years has not been long enough for people to accept Jesus' teaching: "If someone strikes you on the right cheek, turn to him the other also!"; instead, they keep to the Old Testament: "A life for a life, an eye for an eye, a tooth for a tooth...." Hence, will the vengeance be equally horrifying? Evil-doing breeds vengeance, vengeance breeds evil-doing. Horror is extinguished with horror ... is extinguished with horror ... is extinguished with horror. ... The debts can never be repaid. Yet all human experience to the present day declares to us that human beings are powerless against the desire to attempt to repay them.

In Šehovići near Tuzla, a camp has been created for girls between the ages of fourteen and eighteen, to serve the pleasure of the Chetniks.

Enough.

9 July 1992

At last, humanitarian aid. They're not UN packets, but they are American! We were terribly excited and happy. Mom stood in line, and I fluttered around, helping the neighbours to carry home their packets, hardly able to wait for Mom, too, to finally pick up ours. And when we brought them home, all three of us – the two of us plus Grandma – we all spoke at once. Each of us had her own idea of what to do with the grub. All the same, we waited for Dad to come home from work so we could open the packets together. Like on New Year's Eve *[in officially atheistic Communist Yugoslavia, New Year's replaced Christmas as the annual gift-exchanging holiday]* – we wait for midnight for everyone to open their gifts, even though they've in fact been lying under the tree since eight in the evening.

Sorrow and grief. Humiliation. Penury *[lit.* sankiloterija *– the condition of the* sans-culottes, *the unwashed masses of the French Revolution] – fukara*, as we say here. We were so thrilled. About what? About American food packets intended for the United States Army – the soldiers use them when they're off to the battlefield, at least that's what people say. Grey bags made of thick plastic, and inside them a whole collection of little grey or olive-drab plastic bags and one or two wrapped packages with an "entrée" or dessert and in which, in turn, are other plastic bags, this time thicker and exclusively olive-drab, with variously named contents – what they taste like, we have yet to see. The inevitable little bags of coffee, sugar, salt, toilet paper, matches, and moist towelettes.

I don't remember ever being so thrilled about anything as I was about these packets, but now, some ten hours later, the thought of that joy of mine makes me despair – have I and my family sunk as far as this? We who used to enjoy caviar and shellfish, fine cheeses and wines, fresh vegetables and rare steaks, all sorts of pastries and exotic fruits, now we are grateful for charity in the form of ready-to-eat food, packaged who knows when, and crammed with preservatives.

But we have no food any more, and what we got today was manna from heaven.

THE WASHINGTON POST, JULY 10, 1992

Bush Turns Aside Bosnian Plea for Military Intervention

Western Allies at Helsinki Summit Favor More Action

By Don Oberdorfer and Marc Fisher

10 July 1992

... A radio news report: a woman from Višegrad or Foča – I'm not sure, I didn't hear the beginning – is talking about the grisly slapping sound made by the bodies of slain victims that were being flung from the bridge into the river Drina. The people had been ordered to strip, and then they were slaughtered one by one like kurbans *[a kurban is a lamb or kid or calf ritually slaughtered by Muslims on the feast of Kurban-bajram, at the end of the Ramadan fast]* and their bodies thrown into the river. Mom says that they were doing the same thing back in '41 when, on the feast of Bajram, eighty-four Muslims were massacred on the bridge at Foča. That was in December of 1941, and she was an eyewitness. The tradition,

57

therefore, lives on – the fathers charged their sons with this duty: kill a Muslim as soon as the opportunity presents itself. And I believed for thirty years that there were no Chetniks any more. That's what I was taught in school and that's what I lived by: "brotherhood and unity" – a pipe dream or a vile deceit?

Today in the GRAS [*city transit*] buses, dumdum bullets and anti-artillery guns killed three and wounded eight.

In Dobrinja, four were killed and forty wounded.

Now, around 7 p.m., the shelling has once again intensified. The shells are falling very close by.

People are not satisfied with the aid packets: they were expecting oil, flour, sugar, canned meat and fish. In some city wards, packets like this, the so-called family packs, were distributed, but only 5,000 of them in total arrived. What we got was a pure hoax, and overall, the aid that has reached Sarajevo has not yet managed to meet even the daily requirement of the city.

THE WASHINGTON POST, JULY 11, 1992

West Sends In Cavalry, But After Bosnia Is Gone

By Blaine Harden
Washington Post Foreign Service

months after Serbs launched and, by many measures, won a war to annex most of Bosnia and forcibly

12 July 1992

In the course of the day, seven people have been killed in Sarajevo, and ten injured, mostly from shells fired from artillery ostensibly under the control of UNPROFOR. Of those killed, four were children.

There is no running water, not even in the basement.

The power went off around 7 p.m.

1 7 J u l y 1 9 9 2

One more Friday. One more week of war behind us and who knows how many before us.

Douglas Hurd, minister of foreign affairs of Great Britain – in Sarajevo. He says that none other than a sovereign and undivided Bosnia-Herzegovina can be the objective of any negotiations. Thanks for sharing. Bravo! But as things stand, the only chance it has of staying undivided is if all the interested parties change the world, and by God, that's no small feat. Both the big assholes and the little ones are hankering after a chunk of it.

While Hurd was prattling on in the Presidency, fifty metres away from that same Presidency, on the corner of King Tomislav Street and Tito Street, a bomb exploded. One person was killed and fifteen were injured.

I want to go home to Alifakovac. I miss my cats. I know it's idiotic, but I really do miss them, and every time I think of them, I feel a pang. I'm afraid that I have betrayed them, just as everything that I believed in has betrayed me.

As for our tom, our good old Milivoj, I won't have a chance to receive his forgiveness. […] Bedra saw him die. He was walking slowly across the garden and just collapsed – and stayed that way. Maybe it was a stroke, but maybe it was hunger. He was eleven years of age, he was old, and perhaps he wouldn't have lived any longer even in the best of circumstances. All the same, I feel sorry for him. We betrayed him. Abandoned him. Left him to drop dead of starvation. Muši and Vasko are still hanging on, though Muši is horribly thin and Raja says he won't eat anything.

2 2 J u l y 1 9 9 2

It seems to me that I'm beginning to flee from what is happening around me – I'm turning inwards, towards my own problems and dilemmas which have nothing to do with the war. As though I'm shutting myself off from reality. As a matter of fact, that reality is taking on a whole new dimension: in the glitter of glass on the sidewalk – I'm discovering beauty; in the horrific experiences of tormented people – ideas for short stories; in the gradual extinction of my city – a reason for the gentle expiring of my own intellect. In my good luck at eluding death at least three times so far [...] I find justification for throwing caution to the winds and tempting fate.

But perhaps the issue is much less complicated, perhaps I have simply become accustomed to this war and have accepted it as a completely normal way of life. If that's so, then it's not clear to me why I am still writing a diary, for I did not do that before.

THE GLOBE AND MAIL, JULY 23, 1992

23 July 1992

We still don't know what's become of Sudo. B. hasn't had any news of him for eight days already; Ilona and I, on the other hand, have obtained three conflicting reports about him:

1. that he's alive and well and in his apartment in Grbavica,
2. that they've taken him away,
3. that they've taken him away and returned him.

I haven't said anything to B. What should I tell him, when these are all unreliable reports, and anyhow, there's nothing he can do – he himself has been making inquiries in all sorts of places these last few days, but he hasn't got any concrete reply.

I was back home in Alifakovac. I would love to move back up there, but my family tells me that besides being dangerous, which by now doesn't matter at all to me, it's also impractical – on account of food. I would have to take with me some of our wretchedly meagre rations, which are too small to divide. It's always easier to make something for five, because you can streeeeetch out one can of food over three days, and use the leftovers from yesterday, and so on.

Muši showed up, skinny and light as a two-month-old kitten. Vasko didn't turn up, but Raja says that he's alive and well.

Mika told me a grisly tale: the dogs and cats of her neighbourhood (Soukbunar) have become visibly fatter in the past two weeks. Probably on a diet of corpses, because in the immediate vicinity of their home, in some woods less than a hundred metres away, there had been a Chetnik position, and the successful Operation "Fleur-de-lis" *[the device on the Bosnian flag]* of a little while ago left behind many dead that could not be buried, for those woods, it seems, are now a no-man's land.

I have the distinct impression that half of the world's fleet is in the Adriatic by now. At this rate, tomorrow we'll be dipping our feet in sea water, because this flotilla of monster-boats, including the *Iwo Jima*, is bound to force out the last drop of water from the Adriatic basin, and the overflow may well reach all the way to us. Now if only all those battleships, aircraft carriers and assorted flotsam actually felt like doing something*.

I forgot to mention that our house in Alifakovac has got new tenants – Haso and his whole family have moved in with Raja, because their home was badly damaged and is almost uninhabitable.

26 July 1992

There's nothing I can do to rid myself of the grief that has been choking me since yesterday. I cannot comprehend, I cannot accept that Yasmin *[the son of Elma's aunt Raja]* is dead. He's gone. He's buried under two metres of earth. He was life itself, fullness, abundance, joy.

But one day, even to his own parents, he will seem like a dream.

Seven and a half thousand children in Bosnia-Herzegovina will, according to current estimates, remain permanent invalids. Seven and a half thousand

---

*They were in fact deployed to help enforce the economic sanctions against Serbia.

in four and a half months! This land has endured all manner of horrors through its history, but never before now has it been trodden by more lame than hale people, yet it appears that this time is approaching. Already I am encountering the maimed in the street: in wheelchairs – with both legs missing; on crutches – with legs cut off below the ankle or knee or hip. Missing arms, or several fingers or whole hands, with scars, their stumps wrapped in white bandages, empty sleeves and empty trouser legs. It scares me – it seems to me that when it's all over, this will be an accursed city of cripples who will drift like ghosts amid the ruins. And their single purpose will be just this: to drift amid the ruins.

27 July 1992

Beneath the azure sky of Barcelona – the Olympics. The twenty-fifth in the series began the twenty-fifth of July, 1992. I don't know how it came about, but we had electricity and we managed to watch the opening ceremonies. All those people in the audience seemed to me to come from another planet. The first reaction I had, when I saw the packed stadium, was dread, because it occurred to me – what if a shell lands! And once this ghastly anxiety lodged itself within me at the first sight of the stadium, there was no longer anything that could drive it out of me. Not the whole beautiful, fashionable, joyous and contented crowd. Not the overjoyed participants in their colourful uniforms, not the glamorous performance, not the spectacular divas singing arias from popular operas.

And here: death, starvation, horror. Yes, once upon a time there were Olympics in Sarajevo.

29 July 1992

Sudo really was taken away. The fact has been confirmed. Nothing is known about him. It's not known who took him away, where, why, what they intend to do with him. The only thing definite is that he didn't bring his insulin along with him – he didn't want to, he said that he wouldn't be needing insulin any more. B. found out that he was taken away nine days after the fact, and had him immediately put on the list of twelve old men to be exchanged (Sudo, it appears, was the youngest among them – and he's eighty). That list is already in Geneva, but that doesn't mean anything, since we don't know who seized him – it might have been any of the local cutthroats who are robbing and killing in Grbavica, and he could equally have been taken away to who knows which of the "private jails" in which people disappear without trace. A list of hostages for exchange is of no help at all in that case.

Is he still alive? We don't know. What do they want with him, assuming he is still alive? No one can imagine. He was a well-known and respected Sarajevo lawyer – why did they take him away? So they could simply kill him, or so they could exchange him for one of their own, and there are still some of them in Sarajevo, or so they could demand a ransom?

Whatever it turns out to be, Sudo has been taken away and I'm afraid that we will never see him again. The last of the grand old men. Oh God, I have thought so many times of my grandfather and remarked to myself that he died at the right time.

31 July 1992

I was awakened this morning by a hideous booming. It was not the usual explosions that we've by now got accustomed to. For instance, three, four, five, six, or X number of individual explosions one after another do not induce the same kind of terror and sense of helplessness as does that continuous booming that just would not let up all morning, but instead would only approach and recede, in waves. In just the same way the fear, in waves, engulfs you and withdraws. They say that's the cannon. And, you see, there's just no way that I can get used to that sound. Everything echoes with it – the air, the asphalt, the houses, the floor, the walls, the bed on which I'm lying and scribbling this. It's echoing in my chest and in my belly. It's been like that all day.

I went out on the balcony off Grandpa's bedroom, and in the spectacular morning, fresh and clear, I listened to the twittering of the birds in the birch tree in front of the house and the booming and explosions which were tracing out exactly a semi-circle along the rim of the city: Sedrenik, Vratnik, Vasin-han, Babića-bašta, Bistrik, Širokača, Soukbunar.

Today in Sarajevo there were seventy-eight wounded and eleven dead. One of those eleven was killed before my eyes! [...] The man died five paces in front of me! I heard shooting which I didn't even pay attention to, and then I saw the man fall in front of me. I took one more step and then stopped – I couldn't for the life of me figure out why he had fallen. The street was deserted because the bombs had been falling in earnest from early morning. The only people to be found outside were idiots like me (I didn't need to go to work that day at all – the Jewish Community Centre would certainly have survived without me!) and the odd miserable unfortunate. Anyway, on the far side of the pedestrian crossing – the man had fallen on the crossing on Kulović Street, where it enters Tito Street – stood a young man who shouted at me, "Stop, girl! Can't you see that a sniper killed the man!" For as a matter of fact, I had started to take another step and was considering what to do with this man who had fallen down so nonsensically! I stood indecisively; then the bullets began to whistle past. Finally I caught on and stayed rooted to the spot. Good God, how could I have been so stupid and careless! For not five days ago on a crossing on that same street, only down by the Post Office Café, a sniper "prodded" me along, and I ran across, quick as lightning and hunched over as far as possible, and took cover behind the theatre.

So there I stood, sheltered behind the corner of the building that the Veselin Masleša bookstore is in; there across the road from me was the young man who probably saved my life and another greying, older man. Behind me I heard a woman wailing, as if under her breath, "Oh my God, oh my God, they've killed a man! Look, there's his blood! Oh my God...." And another woman, probably younger, judging by her voice, was saying to her, "Shush, quiet, don't look over there. Come on, let's go back. Come on, why have you stopped...." After that I heard someone just above my head, to my right, saying, "Listen, everyone, we have to pull him away from there, maybe he's still alive."

What to do now: stand here and look at that body; run across the street; go back home; or help get him out of danger? The older man from the other side of the street ran across! I did the same before I was at all aware that I was doing it!

France is supporting the establishment of safe havens for refugees within Bosnia-Herzegovina itself. Bravo! All we need is to legalize the ethnic cleansing and genocide that have been going on for as long as they have been and everything will be fine. What France is offering is precisely what Karadžić wants and what he was constantly insisting on in Lisbon.

Europeans are watching the annihilation of the Bosnian Muslims; and beasts that they are, they're offering them as the sole solution and greatest possible aid – a ghetto. All in all, Europe certainly has a wealth of experience with ghettos – no one knows that better than the Jews. Will there be three ghettos? How many will there be in Bosnia when all of this is somehow brought to a close? Will they be enclosed in barbed wire? Well, maybe our European benefactors could come up with a teeny bit of wire and neatly arrange all of us, like monkeys, in our own little cages, and all this for the sake of our security, of the peace of mind of all humanity, and of the various interests of the global powers, great and small.

1 August 1992

Yesterday, on Kozja *[Goat]* bridge, six Serbs were slaughtered. No one knows who did it.

Today on the highway cloverleaf at Stup, around 6:30 p.m., a bus which set out with fifty children from an orphanage who were on their way to Germany was riddled with bullets. Two babies were killed. A large number of the children were babies – they had been tied by sheets or diapers to their seats so that they wouldn't fall out of them during the ride. Thanks to the coverage by German TV, we could follow the departure of the bus, its ride, and the moment of panic which set in after the bus was hit. The entire operation had been undertaken in collaboration with a humanitarian organization from Aachen which had offered to take in the children. Who is responsible, besides the killers, of course, for the fact that what happened happened is unknown. Everyone who was involved in organizing this operation is washing their hands of it and shifting the blame elsewhere.

Our food situation is still bad and getting worse. We're nibbling away at the aid rations in bits. In tiny, tiny bits. Yesterday we ate the last of the noodles, and today we had another of Mom's phenomenal soups. I can't for the life of me figure out what she puts in it when there are none of the things that she would need for a proper soup. We have no oil, no Vegeta [spice mix], no tomatoes – I mean tomato paste. There's salt, there's water, there's flour, and occasionally, there are some herbs, à la stinging nettle, and a bit of beetroot – which Raja sends us from her garden.

4 August 1992

In the Jewish Community Centre, bedlam. People have been coming to see whether they're on the departure list. It's a scene out of a movie: Paris, World War II, the Germans at the city gates, shadowy corridors and stairways packed with desperate people waiting for a visa to Lisbon or to who knows what more fortunate destination. That's how it was in the centre – a dark hallway, a crush of people waiting, fidgeting, exhausted by the interminable standing, the heat, the despair. On their faces a look of total conviction that they personally, above everyone else, have the right to leave this hell. The haughty stand next to the servile, the impatient next to the patient, the hysterical next to the apparently unconcerned. Those who have spent their whole lives demanding are now begging, those who have never had the nerve to demand are now aggressively insisting. And even those who have never been able to ask anyone for any sort of favour are now doing so, and you can see how uncomfortable it makes them. Some are certain that they will leave on the first plane. Tormented people who perhaps have lost someone, or who have been driven out, or whose home has gone up in flames. [...] But the news is bad: flights have been postponed, and buses are not permitted to transport Muslims – a man and a woman who set out in yesterday's convoy were taken off the bus. The Chetniks forbid it.

8 August 1992

Over the last twenty-four hours in Sarajevo there have been 24 killed and 114 injured.

In Bosnia-Herzegovina, 31 dead and 250 injured (this includes Sarajevo).

I arrived too late for yet another bomb. I was in the middle of Drvenija Bridge when the explosion resounded by the College of Art. Was there a hundred metres between us? More or less? – it doesn't matter. In any case our lives depend on the length and frequency of our steps. Sometimes it's good to run, at other times it's better to be slow. A colleague of mine whom I chanced upon recently just about showered me with kisses in the middle of the street because, as she puts it, she owes her life to my mother. She met Mom in Vaso Miskin Street. She was not at all comfortable with the idea of lingering there, because Vaso Miskin gets shelled every few minutes: there are always injuries, and almost every time fatalities as well. Nevertheless, out of respect for an older colleague she did stop, and they stood there talking, she says, not even half a minute, before she hurried on her way. That half a minute saved her life. In just that amount of time she would have arrived precisely in position for a mortar shell. Mom was going in the opposite direction – in other words, she was moving away from the bomb. I told Mom this story, and she said she remembered meeting Danka, but she has no recollection at all of a bomb landing anywhere in the vicinity on that day.

14 August 1992

The desperate staff of the old-age home in Nedarici are making appeals for food delivery and the removal of corpses. The old folks no longer have

67

anything to eat. They are dying of hunger and exhaustion. There's no electricity, there's no water – is there anything more horrible, sadder, more degrading than an old-age home without water? The bodies of five old people have been decomposing in the basement for several days now. Out of the 150 residents that there were at the beginning of the war, which would be the fourth of April, there are now 94 left.

15 August 1992

A full ten days without electricity. I don't think I've as yet talked about how we cook without electricity and without gas. Well, both we and everyone else in the building, except for Ruža, cook at the Mrgans'. The Mrgans and the Dukas have gas, but none of the neighbours want to bother the Dukas – both of them are old and ill, and let's not even speak of the grief that oppresses them.

In the morning, at noon, and in the late afternoon, a parade up and down the stairs gets underway. The ladies of the house carry up and down pots and pans, noodles or peas, spices, if one of them still has any, tea, water (water is precious – there isn't any, so everybody brings along her own). And then everyone waits her turn at Safeta's. A whole crew of housewives in one place – sometimes there'll be five or six of them, all standing around the stove and minding the pots, either their own or someone else's, with spoons and ladles, dishcloths and lids in their hands, aprons around their waists, wearing fuzzy slippers, plastic slippers, knitted ones, or flip-flops. They carry on conversations, give advice and recipes, add things, take things away. There's the buzzing of voices and the clanging of pans. If anyone supposes that there's any drinking of coffee here, they're mistaken – there's no coffee any more for such "pointless" drinking.

Safeta, naturally, is the head cook – after all, this is all going on in her kitchen. She lets people in and sees them out, minds the stove, tastes and advises. I've learned all kinds of things from her, and from the others, as I've boiled water for tea.

Now, when there's no bread and no electricity, then it's a bit dicey, because Safeta doesn't have a gas oven. In that case, Zora occasionally, but only occasionally, heats up the *tiš-šporet [a type of solid-fuel oven with stove]* (fuel needs to be hoarded for winter), and bread is baked in her kitchen.

And when even that isn't possible, well then, back at Safeta's, the women fry fritters – whoever has cooking oil. What the ones who don't have oil do, I don't know. We have been lucky – for several days we were completely out, but then we got some in a delivery at the Jewish Community Centre.

There's quite the to-do when water arrives – in the basement. The first person to notice it runs downstairs with buckets, canisters, bottles, pans. The people on the sixth floor haul the water up by a rope – one person in the basement does the filling, another does the pulling, a third pours it out into the bathtub. Shouts go back and forth: "Pull!" "Fill it up!" "Hurry up!" And: "Hey, wait your turn!" That's V. yelling from the sixth floor. The low-life!

So there we go, the four of us, up and down from the fifth floor who knows how many times, carrying twenty to thirty litres of water each time. We have to fill up our entire array of buckets and pails, cans, pans, pots and bottles. We don't keep water in the bathtub because it would make washing very awkward (our sink is broken); so instead, we have a huge metal tub that holds 100 litres, and by the time we fill it up along with everything else ... need I say more....

18 August 1992

Today is my birthday. My thirty-first! Congratulations! Thank you.

23 August 1992

Sudo is dead. The first to get the news were Munir's family. The telephone rang, and when they lifted the receiver, from the other end of the line came a question: "Does Grbavica mean anything to you?" I don't know which one of them answered, but whoever it was managed to collect himself and answer, "It does." There followed a brief pause, and then: "He's not alive any more. His wife is alive." And the caller hung up. Who called, how he knew, where he was calling from, why he didn't identify himself – we can only guess. Was what we heard today true? [...] To be honest, I don't believe he is alive, and from the first moment that I heard he had been taken away, I didn't believe he would survive, because his chances were, let's face it, nil – eighty years old, a diabetic without insulin, a Muslim, and a prominent one, in the hands of the Chetniks.

Nevertheless I won't mourn yet. I won't hope either, I won't think about it any more, not until it's definite, absolutely certain, one way or the other.

Today in the city, fourteen dead – in Daira gardens alone, in a queue for water, eight dead and eight injured. Among the dead, one baby.

2 5   A u g u s t   1 9 9 2

Today the streets were almost empty. In the air, on people's faces, in the Jewish Community Centre, in the apartment building – an appalling tension. Everyone's waiting for something. In actuality, everyone's waiting for death.

The municipal government has passed a resolution that, until further notice, the law making attendance at work mandatory is suspended, in order to reduce people's exposure to risk as much as possible in the next few days, when a massive offensive and heavy shelling of the city are expected.

The *Oslobođenje ["Liberation," the Sarajevo daily newspaper]* building has burned to the ground. From a building of that size only a few basement rooms have remained intact. Nevertheless, *Oslobođenje* came out again today – mind you, only four pages' worth and in a very limited edition, and I didn't manage to buy a copy, but nevertheless, it did come out. Out of spite.

The National Library* is burning! They've set fire to the National Library. Firefighters from all over the city are putting it out, but the criminals are keeping up the bombardment. It will burn down too! It will burn down the way the Post Office burned down, the way the *Oslobođenje* building did! The National Library, without which you couldn't imagine a postcard of Sarajevo.

27 August 1992

Bombs fell again today, but I outran them. More precisely, I ran between them. Before work I had gone to trade in some *[Yugoslav]* dinars for *[Bosnian]* coupons. The bank across from the College of Art was crowded. I had just made it to the front of the line when there was an explosion somewhere very close by. The teller jumped out of her chair, gave me an ashen and bewildered stare, then sat back down and resumed counting the bills. I felt the terror flowing out of my stomach, and my feet and hands going numb. I heard the commotion of the crowd behind me, and I didn't need to turn around to look at their faces – I felt the weight of their panic on the nape of my neck; their fear was choking me more than my own. I hate being stuck in a crowd, especially one in distress, yet there I was. I didn't know what to do, and then the second one struck. Two women made a mad rush into the bank. I took a look at the roof above me – glass. I decided to run outside before the third one hit, because the second one was closer than the previous one. I ran as fast as my legs could take me, dashed past the First Gymnasium and across Drvenija, and no sooner had I ducked around the corner of the former Women's Gymnasium than along came number three. The third one struck the First Gymnasium, the second had landed in the courtyard of the former Women's Gymnasium, and the first on the Papagajka *[the Parrot, the popular nickname of a new building noted for its garish colour scheme]*. The first one had shattered the thick glass on the main doors of the JCC, and one fragment had injured

*Also called *Vjećnica*, "City Hall."

71

someone (not seriously, a cut on the thigh), with the result that when I flew into the JCC, scared out of my wits, there was quite a sight to greet me – glass and blood all over the floor.

[...] I'm in the basement. And at this moment, for the first time in five months, it has hit me that I'm living in a war! I did, of course, know that, but only now have "the scales fallen from my eyes." While watching the wavering shadows that the light from the candle is sending across the basement walls, I came, dumbfounded, to the realization that around me there is a war, that I am in a chilly, damp, and stinking basement, that surrounding me are unfortunates who have already been driven mad by five months of anxiety and desperate efforts to survive.

I don't know how to describe the basement wall on which, a few minutes ago, in a moment of lucidity and courage, I read the truth which has hammered all its terror into three letters – w-a-r. On that wall I saw written out a novel about a colony of basement-dwelling creatures who have only one goal – to go on living as long as possible in the dankness, airlessness, and stench of their habitat.

In this basement there is something romantic, something mystical, to put it simply, it has its own spell. Every time I lie on the trunk in our storage locker (the locker is 1.6 metres wide, and the trunk is 1.4 metres long) and I gaze through the wooden slats towards the basement across which flickers the faint light of a candle that is already burning down, I feel as though I'm in the hold of an old clipper ship. And I don't need anything more than that – a tale starts to unfold of its own accord, and I find myself starting to take pleasure in that ambience.

28 August 1992, the 146th Day of the War

Today I spoke with a young woman who works in the National Library. She said that they have been putting the books away since April, but that they have managed to store only a small fraction of them. The most precious books and manuscripts, as well as the so-called *Bosniaca* – a corpus of works that originated in Bosnia or else have to do with Bosnia – have already been put away. The National Library, more precisely, the University Library, had repeatedly requested the authorities to assign them one of the atomic bomb shelters (which aren't being used anyway) to store the books in, but the authorities didn't even blink, let alone act.

We simply don't know how many millions of books went up in flames. The university library held about 3.6 million titles; but what the *exact* number was, even the university had no idea. As to how many exactly were burned, they have no idea, but we're talking millions.

1 September 1992

The one-hundred-fiftieth day of the war in Sarajevo: this morning at 6:30, between the barking of the machine guns and the distant resounding of the cannons, I caught sight, in the sky, of a white dove. Splendid, white as snow, elegant, with a small head, an elongated spindle-shaped body and delicate, finely traced wings, it flew before my eyes as though it wasn't real. As it soared into the heavens and rose above the shadows of the surrounding buildings, it caught the sun's rays and gleamed golden.

Was it an omen?

Dragan says that a white dove flying heavenwards is a sign that someone's soul is departing for paradise. Oh, there are too many, too many departing for paradise these days.

It's already our twenty-sixth day without electricity.

4 September 1992

I don't think I've written anything yet about the pitch darkness of our nights. At the beginning of the war we had some fifty candles. Now they're gone. In the evenings we sit in the kitchen, and by seven-thirty already we're watching the tiny flame of the oil lamp which is just bright enough to chase the darkness away from the table. We chat a little, but we do that to keep up appearances – mostly we drink in the light from that flickering spark and each one of us weaves an inner story of our own, mute and bitter. We don't sit for long – an hour and a half, two at the most – we're conserving the oil. Nevertheless, we don't find it hard to go to bed at such an early hour, because in the pitch darkness sleepiness overtakes us and by half past nine or ten we are already in bed. And each of us enters the world of sleep with the hope of waking to see another day.

7 September 1992

Elegantly dressed and made-up ladies on their way to work in the morning are carrying – instead of purses – flasks, bottles, and pails for water. In the afternoon, dressed casually and carrying large buckets and canisters, they'll set out with their husbands for a stroll to the nearest fountain. The water bucket – the latest fashion statement. These days this accessory is a must for the trendy Sarajevan.

We here on Radičević Street are still lucky, that is to say, we have been lucky – water has been reaching our basement, and occasionally it's made it up as far as the fifth floor; whereas for a month and a half already, the inhabitants of Mejtaš have had to make their way down from their hilltop to one of the basements in the city centre or else to one of the wells which are always enormously crowded. And then, slowly, weighed down with twenty or thirty litres of water, or even more if they have some suitable conveyance, it's back home, uphill, step by step. And August is – a Sarajevo August. The last few days people have been almost relieved to go down to the basement, where it's cool.

The preparations for Sefarad '92 *[the celebration of the five-hundredth anniversary of the arrival of the Sephardic Jews in Sarajevo after their expulsion from Spain]* are in their final stages. The celebration begins on the eleventh of September, and it will be a real cultural event.

8 September 1992

The power has come back on! Unbelievable, after thirty-three days, the doorbell rang again and the lightbulbs lit up. We were taken aback – we'd almost got to the point of not needing electricity any longer. We were quite nonplussed. Someone, as a joke, flipped a switch, and there was a burst of light. You should have seen our dumbfounded expressions, our eyes wide as saucers! We had no idea what to do, so we didn't do anything. We didn't even turn on the TV – what for?

THE NEW YORK TIMES, SEPTEMBER 15, 1992

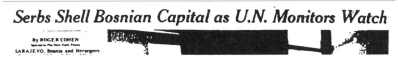

Serbs Shell Bosnian Capital as U.N. Monitors Watch

By ROGER COHEN
SARAJEVO, Bosnia and Herzegov<

17 September 1992

SEFARAD '92 – September 11, 12, 13, and 14. It was an unbelievable event. A step outside our normal life, normal for wartime, anyhow. Holiday Inn, distinguished guests, speeches, concerts, tuxedos and gowns, cocktail parties! I felt as though I had stepped into some parallel universe; I could scarcely believe that everything that was happening was – reality.

Yesterday, the departure of another convoy organized by the Jewish Community Centre. One hundred and fifty-six people left Sarajevo. In the morning, before the departure – bedlam, emotion. Those who are leaving are in tears; so are those remaining behind. Their faces swollen from weeping. The question that was hovering in the air all that morning – will we ever see each other again? When will that be? Where?

20 October 1992

The hundred ninety-ninth day since the first bomb fell on Sarajevo and almost a month since I last wrote anything in my diary. I couldn't: I had neither will nor electricity nor candles. There has been no electricity for two months now, with one brief interruption of some six or seven dazzlingly bright nights. No running water either – water cannot be pumped from Bačevo, which supplies 70% of the city's requirements, unless there is electricity.

At our place in Alifakovac there was water, since our supply comes from sources in Bistrik, so I along with my family dragged home as much water as I could every day.

People start to gather as early as 5 a.m. at the wells, fountains, and hydrants on the slopes of the city. At the fountain by the "Seven Brothers"* there is always a crowd, and it's no better at the hydrants by the church of St. Anthony all the way to the top of Ćolin Potok or to Alifakovac. Water is hauled in canisters, buckets, casks, bottles, by hand, in backpacks or in carts that come in the most unlikely models: from children's wagons to airport and supermarket buggies, to mini-sidecars that people pull themselves, and various *self-made [sic]* contraptions.

People have begun to defecate in parks or in plastic bags which they then throw into dumpsters or on the trash heaps which are building up on the sidewalks, because they simply cannot transport enough water for all their needs – for drinking, cooking, personal hygiene, laundry, and pouring down the toilet, especially when they live in apartments in tall high-rises (the elevators, of course, are not working) and in large families. There are various systems of water utilization: dirty water is collected for pouring down the toilet, when washing your hair you collect the water with which you wet your hair and use it for the first rinse, you collect the water from the second rinse and use it to rinse the soap from your body, and the like. However, no matter how much you conserve it, there's never enough. People lose their lives at the fountains. The mother of my friend S.P. was killed in a queue for water, and N.V. died on the way to a fountain.

The parks are ending up without trees – it's winter, there's no fuel,

---

*The Seven Brothers, legendary figures from the Turkish period, have given their name to the fountain in front of the mosque where they are entombed. They also bestow good luck on visitors who toss coins into the fountain.

nothing to cook or heat with. It's only in the morning that you notice that one more tree is missing. Naturally, here too the black market is flourishing – those who have managed somehow to supply their own needs continue to cut down trees in the parks and sell them; one bag, the kind that normally holds thirty kilograms of potatoes, full of wood will cost 30 to 50 Deutschmarks, and that's so little fuel that I don't know what kind of fire you can start with it.

Hunger has leapt at our throats, crept into our homes – among the elderly and children, but also among those in the prime of life. In front of the building that used to be army headquarters and now houses the Egyptian UNPROFOR contingent, hungry people are waiting for the Egyptians to give them the leftovers of their dinner. Our neighbour N.M. told me that up till a month ago, those leftovers were thrown into dumpsters; but after a memo requesting that the food be distributed to the needy, the well-fed soldiers began to hand it out in the courtyard in front of the building. The queue stretched out into the street, up to 200 metres long. People stand two or three abreast and wait four or five hours. And you can find there both destitute refugees and elegantly dressed ladies.

Children swarm around UNPROFOR troop carriers and trucks, and what I experienced in the city slums of India, when I was besieged by beggars and children asking for money and pointing at their mouths in a gesture that meant "give me food," is now happening here, in my city, on my streets, but the children aren't the tiny wide-eyed Indian ragamuffins, but instead pampered city kids, who only eight months ago were hanging out at the corner stores, choosing from the candy counter their favourite treats.

Today I watched as the well-fed foreign soldiers on a truck going down the Street of the Defenders of the City (formerly Yugoslav National Army, don't you know) tossed to the children little packages of sweets. The children were running to catch them, the soldiers were having a great time. The kids who were lucky enough to grab a box of goodies shouted, "Mmmmm, candy! *Hvala ti*, UNPROFOR! Tenk-yu!" I found it hard to take. I felt demeaned and impoverished. I asked myself whether I was certain that no amount of poverty would ever drive me to sell myself to one of the ordinary little soldier-boys who have become here what they could never aspire to be back in their own home towns in Canada: demigods.

28 October 1992

Zora's friend and my acquaintance, Sadija, has lost a leg. A mortar shell flew into her apartment, and she was so badly wounded that they had to amputate her leg below the hip. She's thirty years old.

Gordana K., my friend's sister, was killed on Saturday. She was on her balcony when she was struck by a bullet from a PAM (anti-aircraft gun), and she fell from the fourth floor. She was hit in the head – her head was almost completely blown apart. She was waiting on the balcony, which looks out on Poljine, for her mother to come back from the bakery – that day there had been constant shooting, her mother had been away a long time, and she was probably worried that something might have happened to her – that is the only explanation for why she was on that balcony at all, for it was always closed off, treated as off-limits, precisely because it was the most dangerous place in the whole apartment.

I'm afraid. In ten days, I've been to three places to express my condolences and have two more to go to. Five deaths in my immediate circle, and a young woman I know, a permanent invalid.

4 November 1992

It's terrifying that for months now, night in and night out, I've been sitting by the light of an oil lamp, going to bed about eight in the evening, waking up before five, but getting out of bed after six because only then does the sun rise; that I listen without any particular emotion to the explosions of mortar shells; that I live on rice day in and day out; and that I consider that a true blessing from God. It's terrifying that for months I've read nothing apart from the occasional newspaper article – I do not feel the need to read anything at all, and the most terrifying thing of all is that I accept this, such a condition, as normal.

22 November 1992

A convoy left on the fourteenth of November, but I wasn't on it. Everything was okay, I made it onto the list and I could have left the city, and by now I would probably already be in Israel. Why didn't I go? I don't know. I had one foot in the bus, but the other one was heavier. I don't know. I don't know. But I think the answer closest to the truth is that I can't bear not to see the end of this story. If this story doesn't outlive me. Well, maybe next year in Jerusalem.

7 December 1992

I had a conversation with E.T. He thinks we are on the verge of a war with Croatia and the HVO *[Hrvatsko Vijeće Odbrane = Croatian Defence Council, the militia of the Bosnian Croats]*. He says that military victory resolves nothing. This war, he says, is the result of global machinations – it suits Europe, and America, too, to have 300,000 fewer Muslims, it being a question, quite simply, of a balance of power in some future Parliament. He predicts that the situation will calm down only in the spring of '94. Lucky us. *[HVO soldiers began to come into conflict with the Bosnian government forces in February of 1993. The situation in Sarajevo did indeed calm down in the spring of 1994, as Elma's letters of that period indicate, though, of course, the "peace" proved to be only temporary.]*

9 December 1992

I don't know where the bombs are landing, but I know that this very evening people are dying, and I sense the terror of the souls that are abandoning mangled bodies. And not terror of the unknown they are entering, but of the familiar they are leaving behind. Human souls are everywhere around me, lost and lonely, and radiating from them and penetrating me is a boundless, boundless sorrow. Every corner of this city is haunted by the souls of those who were not ready to leave it, but were so suddenly and cruelly torn away from its streets, its parks, schools, cafés, apartments. This land of Bosnia is full of the souls of weary people who are incapable of grasping why they were so prematurely hurled among their ancestors, when they had not yet even begun to live with the full power of their desires and talents.

THE GLOBE AND MAIL, DECEMBER 29, 1992

Elderly in Sarajevo freezing to death

Severe cold takes toll on nursing-home, UNHCR says; Bosnians hope to end siege

29 December 1992

People are dying of cold and hunger.

The parks of Sarajevo have been laid waste – in the park around the Austrian house not a single tree is standing. The birches along the colonnade that leads to the cable railway no longer exist. The trees lining one side of the boulevard from the market near the National Library to the Hotel National – some 350 metres – are missing. In the park by the kindergarten in the same street – not a single tree, just the day-care building, totally devastated, but not by a mortar shell. People have stripped the roofing and all the wood from the structure: even termites could not have done a better job. People are walking around the city carrying axes and saws. They chop down the massive old shade trees, but also the young saplings, no thicker than your hand. The saddest sight of all is the people who show up late, after some tree has been "executed," and gather the splinters, the sawdust, the twigs, and the bark that have been left behind. They wander around through the devastated parks, with straw bags, plastic bags, baskets, and numb with cold, scoop up the debris.

Desperate people are sifting through trash heaps looking for heating fuel [...] (they say that old Adidas and plastic slippers burn the best). To say nothing of the fact that basements are being cleared of old furniture – by those who have some; those who do not are starting to burn woodwork and furniture that is still in use.

1 1   J a n u a r y   1 9 9 3

During the night in the region surrounding Žepa, seventy people died of hunger and cold, chiefly children and old people.

U.S. Finds Serbs Skimming Bosnia Aid

Continued From Page A1 | United Nations must largely depend on | The Serbs, the report notes, have

1 3   J a n u a r y   1 9 9 3

The death toll from cold and hunger in the region of Žepa, Bratunac, and Srebrenica has reached 490.

1 5   J a n u a r y   1 9 9 3

A shell lands next to the brewery. On the people who are waiting in line for water. Eight dead and twenty injured. I went by there immediately afterwards, but I can't write about it. I've had enough of circling like a vulture around every spot of blood on the streets of this city, describing and recording it. I'm afraid I'll develop a taste for it and start frequenting these banquets of Death. I'm afraid I'll start luxuriating in the depictions of these atrocities. I keep telling myself: I would hate to miss out on even a moment of this horror! Why?

Why didn't I go to Israel? I don't know even that yet. I can't help thinking that my sole motivation is a desire and a need to see what will happen, to be in the middle of things, where the action is. This war is beginning to sit well with me: here I'm close to the depths, and hey, I may as well stop lying to myself, the depths fascinate me tremendously, I want to reach them – that's the experience I've been missing. My whole life I've had it easy: a happy childhood in a happy family, parents who offered me, along with love, everything they had, and who raised me so that I don't ask of them what they don't have to give me. Prohibitions didn't exist for me, nor did any sort of compulsion; I was taught to be independent, all the problems that I had I created for myself. Obviously there was some evil lacking in this life of mine. I studied philosophy and literature, I played sports, I travelled, I played the piano. However, what I discovered in the world outside my family wasn't particularly nice. Well, this "not nice" element was something unknown to me, and I wanted to get to know it. The unknown has always exerted a fascination over me. To experience terror, misery, brushes with death – not for nothing did I dream of becoming a war correspondent, admittedly, when I was seventeen or eighteen. Later I convinced myself that this was irresponsible, childish, even immoral – hadn't I always been taught that one should strive for the good and the beautiful? Yet I longed to encounter misery, to record it, discover it, and reveal it. That wasn't really creative, not especially "activist," and a human being must be a creator. And so it was that I "forgot" about wars and tried to find myself in some sort of well-ordered life and peace that would give me the opportunity to read, reflect, learn, and then to create something. And it didn't come easily to me! In no way! I was missing the other side of life. In my own experience it was missing.

Now I'm living in wartime, I'm stubbornly writing a diary, I have felt terror, I am experiencing misery and I've seen death, and still it's not enough for me! I'm convinced that only now am I actually learning something and that there is probably still a lot more that I need to learn, still a lot of disillusionment that I need to experience in order to level out the peaks and troughs of my existence, so that I can finally arrive at the zero point that will guarantee me the position of the objective observer who will at last be able to discern what humanity is and what the world is about. I'm mad! At the very least, I'm infantile. But I can repeat that to myself 3 million times and I still won't feel any different. I truly am a spoiled child.

THE NEW YORK TIMES, FEBRUARY 21, 1993

Awash in Pain, Sarajevo Is Sinking Into Despair

By JOHN F. BURNS
Special to The New York Times
SARAJEVO, Bosnia and Herzegovi- | when the siege began have been direct

23 February 1993

People continue to die in eastern Bosnia. The Chetniks refuse to let aid convoys with food pass through.

Electricity "drops in" from time to time in various parts of the city. Naturally, not to us.

In New York negotiations concerning Bosnia are continuing. Vance and Owen are proposing ten provinces.

5 March 1993

For several days now the operation to parachute aid into eastern Bosnia has been in effect. The Yanks are dropping pallets of food (one pallet = one ton), but during the first two days not a single packet fell in the besieged towns.

Cerska has fallen. It's being reported on the news that 250 people have been slaughtered!

Negotiations continue. Bravo! In the end everything will be resolved

83

"by peaceful means," that is to say, an utter and deathly stillness will settle over Bosnia, while the Chetniks will go on negotiating with the rest of the world concerning the western boundary of Serbia – somewhere around Washington.

1 5   M a r c h   1 9 9 3

Morillon* is in Srebrenica. He's been there already two or three days. He says he's trying to "save the people of Srebrenica." According to some reports, unofficial ones, of course – who would be announcing this publicly? – our side won't let him make a move to leave, because, they say, Srebrenica is safe as long as Uncle Morillon is visiting.

1 9   M a r c h   1 9 9 3

Today in front of the brewery, an unreal picture: women are rinsing their laundry at the fountains. Huge pans and tubs in improbable colours, and in them underwear, but also sweaters, winter skirts, blankets, rugs. Women in housecoats and plastic slippers. Bare calves gleam. Faces are red from bending over, and the plunging necklines of the housecoats reveal the whiteness of bosoms. It looks as though heads have been planted on the wrong torsoes. I stood and watched and couldn't believe it: in the middle of the city, in the middle of a horrible war, only ten metres from soldiers armed to the teeth, a pastoral scene. They're laughing, they're splashing each other, they're leaping about to dodge the jets of water, they've lifted their long unattractive dresses and tied them in a knot in front, just below the knee. They're playing. One of them is my age, maybe two or three years older. Heavy-set, pale-skinned. Her breasts are swollen, almost falling

*General Philippe Morillon replaced Canadian Lewis MacKenzie as commander of UNPROFOR. For his action on behalf of the people of Srebrenica, he was personally reprimanded by UN Secretary-General Boutros Boutros-Ghali, who accused him of "exceeding his mandate." Soon thereafter, he was recalled to France.

out of her dress; she's vigorously rubbing and rinsing, rising and falling, her hips are dancing left-right, up-down. I wonder whether she's continuing last night's *[bedroom]* dance or whether she is simply attempting to exhaust her lust by washing clothes.

I was over to visit a co-worker who lives in a high-rise on Tito Street. As I'm going up the stairs, I meet a little boy, about five or six years old. He's coming down the stairs humming: "Eighty-four ...." He's sweet, blond, wearing some enormous clunky shoes, holding on with both hands to the balusters of the railing, and he's coming slowly down the stairs, mumbling something. I think to myself – he's counting. I ask him, "What's this eighty-four?" He doesn't answer. I ask again, "Is it eighty-four stairs?" "No," he replies. "Then what's eighty-four?" "It's an eighty-four that hit my mother."*

His mother had been killed some days previously, when the car in which she was riding drove into a burst of gunfire from the "sower of death."

<u>5 April 1993</u>

The 365th day of the war. The first year is behind us.

---

*Apparently the M84, a 152 mm howitzer of Yugoslav design.

85

Letters

One of the few reliable communications links to the outside world for the people of Sarajevo has been ham radio. Soon after the war started, the Jewish Community Centre in Zagreb, Croatia, set up an SOS service for refugees from Sarajevo to speak with friends and relatives they had left behind*.

Through the radio station, Elma found new friends and a wider audience than she could ever have imagined. (She describes her initial encounter with Caka in the letter dated July 17, 1994.) Eventually she was writing letters to Caka, Caka's sister Adica, Dunja Šprajc of the Zagreb JCC, and after February 5, 1994, when Ilona left for Zagreb, to her as well. Caka asked for permission to publish Elma's first letter to her, Adica showed her own translation of it to a journalist who had it published in a newspaper in Sweden, Dunja and Ilona helped turn the letters into a book, and so it went....

When Elma visited Zagreb in July 1994 to see Ilona, she met Dunja and Adica for the first time. Caka had by this time left for Prague with her husband. Adica and her husband were reunited and came to live in Toronto, where Caka joined them in the fall of 1995. (Totally unaware that Elma's writing had reached North America, Adica came across a poster advertising this book while at a publishing conference in June 1995. She in turn amazed us by producing the originals of some of the letters translated in the following pages.)

*Only the ill, the elderly, and women with children under eight were allowed to leave Sarajevo; able-bodied men were considered essential to the war effort and therefore obligated to stay. Many men did eventually find a way out of the city, but in the meantime, there were a lot of separated families.

There was, of course, no regular postal service during the war, so Elma had to rely on foreign journalists or UN personnel to act as her couriers. While waiting for an opportunity to send her letters, she continued to add to them. Hence her letters often consist of several instalments.

Sarajevo, 7 July 1993

Dear friends [letter to the Jelićes, her aunt's family in Zagreb],
It's now forty-five minutes past nine, "quarter to ten" by today's reckoning *[her word for "quarter" is* "frtalj" = "Viertel," *a trendy Germanism].* I'm sitting in the kitchen and using up the last drops of petroleum in a home-made lamp – a small jar of Fructal brand baby food, containing diesel fuel with a pinch of salt added – to reduce the smoke – and a wick pulled through the lid. The jar is standing under a cylinder made from a bottle of Meinle egg liqueur whose bottom has been cut out, and the whole thing is standing in a glass ashtray with the erstwhile crest of Bosnia-Herzegovina which someone sometime swiped from the erstwhile Parliament. The contraption is very handy, and it even looks nice.

First: what does it mean to sit in our kitchen in these times in these spaces?

It means taking the risk that a piece of shrapnel from a sudden mortar shell might smash through the tile and Arborite of our improvised kitchen and interrupt the writing of this letter, and turn my life into a death notice *[notices bearing the name, dates, and likeness of the deceased posted on walls, telephone poles, etc., rather like our lost-and-found signs]* – its text typed by the hand of one of my loved ones and photocopied ten times over for the ten corners of this city. There exists, of course, a more fortunate possibility – that I lose a hand or some other trifle of my anatomy. We already have one hole from such a piece of shrapnel on the kitchen ceiling. It is not my wish to frighten you or fascinate you, I'm merely trying to illustrate for you life in Sarajevo.

Secondly: what does it mean to use up the last drops of diesel fuel?

Most simply put, it means that for the time being we will be groping around in the dark unless I manage to get hold of three litres tomorrow. I

87

do know, of course, that there are such things as oil lamps, but we don't have enough *[cooking]* oil to be able to afford to turn it into smoke, even to produce light by those means.

Somewhere a shell has just fallen, but not close enough to make me withdraw to the "safety" of a lower floor. But that shell might have landed in somebody's apartment and blown up its safest nook and killed a sleeping family. In Sarajevo there is no safe place. But Sarajevans have by now gotten used to that and it is generally acknowledged that one cannot escape fate. After at least a hundred incredible stories of nonsensical deaths of absolutely innocent people, I too acknowledge: one cannot escape fate.

Perhaps this statement sounds defeatist to you, but thanks to it life here manages to flow on.

I've lit up a cigarette: the Sarajevo brand Drina in paper wrapping without any markings and without cellophane. Today at the Markale market a pack like this went for 10 DM, on the black market, of course. Obviously, I didn't spend 10 marks for a pack of cigarettes: I have the good fortune to work for a company that pays us with a few cigarettes along with our regular wages. Otherwise, the official price of a carton of cigarettes is 400,000 coupons, and my last month's wages (in June) were 300,000. At that time a carton cost 200,000, [one carton = 10 packs = 200 cigarettes] so my entire wages could buy me fifteen packs. As a matter of fact, my earnings are among the best in the city – at least twice as much as my mother's. As for pensioners – don't ask. Everything is traded for cigarettes and cigarettes are traded for everything. Cigarettes are currency. You should know that this nicotine product is unavailable in the open market; it can be bought only through the company you work for, and in this city most people are out of work.

The black market is thriving. Everyone dabbles in it. I, for instance, go to the market and trade cigarettes for cotton batting *[a cheap substitute for sanitary napkins]* or else I sell the cigarettes (mind you, I don't stand in the marketplace; instead, I do it more elegantly – I give them to someone else to sell in exchange for a 20% cut) and then I buy facial cream, which costs, on the average, 4 DM. A 400-gram tin of canned food cost 25

DM today, a kilogram of onions went for 10, half a kilogram of powdered milk, 25 DM, etc., etc.

Of all the people I know my parents are the only ones who have not as yet bought, let alone sold, anything on the black market.

Black marketeering in food is a crime for which a sufficiently horrible punishment does not exist. Food from humanitarian aid shipments turns up first in the market and only then in the regular rations. Some food staples never reach those for whom they are intended – a few days ago butter appeared in the market. I still haven't heard of anyone I know receiving butter in their aid rations even though the package had UNHCR markings. I myself have counted in various trash heaps an even six crates of completely rotten oranges. Oranges were being distributed to the elderly and to children, two per aid handout, and this happened, it seems to me, all told, two or three times. Now don't imagine that the oranges went bad in the course of transport – in that case they wouldn't turn up in trash heaps on city sidewalks. They rotted in black marketeers' dens because they didn't manage to sell them for *dojč marke [Deutschmarks]*. And there are people literally dying of hunger. A huge number of children are malnourished, and today I ran into an acquaintance, a mechanical engineer, a Ph.D., forty-two years old, who is in despair because he doesn't have a particle of flour in the house. It's been two weeks since there's been any bread in the whole city. Simply put, there is no bread for sale in the grocery stores, and the private bakeries produce exclusively for the army. Think what it would be like if tomorrow in all of Zagreb you couldn't find one single loaf of bread. And the same thing the next day, and the day after that, and the sixteenth day after that. There is no bread because in all the city *[let alone in the bakeries]* there has been no – and I mean *no* – electricity or water or gas for more than three weeks.

I do not feel sorry for myself, I do not complain. It doesn't occur to me to evoke sympathy or outrage. And to say it again, I'm not trying to scare you. This is life here. Our life. A very human life whose protagonists are only human. And nothing more and nothing less than human. People the way people are – good or bad, brave or cowardly, rebels or boot lickers, thieves or honest people, victims or butchers, fanatics or sceptics, or sceptical fanatics and fanatical sceptics. On the fifth of April of last year I began to play the chronicler. I kept a diary regularly every day. I recorded a mass of news reports and my own experiences. I kept the diary very carefully, very precisely for some eight months, and then I got sick of it. To put it crudely – the war was no longer something to put oneself out for.

The war became a lifestyle. At least for me. I adapt easily, I don't burden myself with unnecessary principles. I have never yet in my life said that *a priori* there exists an act that I could not bring myself to perform. As far as I can recall in my own life, I have always placed myself in a position to choose and I could permit myself to adapt as well. Naturally, I can credit such a way of life to the fact that I have never had any real troubles. [...] I could have left before the war or during it. I chose to stay and to accept the consequences of that choice. This war has not lain heavily on me. I could not permit myself to pass up an experience like this. If the meaning of life is not the search for meaning, then what is it? And you cannot say that you have tried to discover its meaning if you have cut yourself off from any aspect of it that might contribute to it.

I'm sharing with you all these wearisome and perhaps unedifying reflections in order to convince you that this is not the materialization of my despair or my bitterness. This is my need to recapitulate my wartime experience, and for that I require a listener, not a conversational partner, just a listener. For you and I cannot discuss this war. Nowadays we inhabit different worlds, you and I. We do not understand each other and in certain matters we will not only never understand each other, but there will also be times when we won't be able to communicate at all because we will be speaking different languages. Nevertheless, that does not diminish my need and my duty to tell you something about this war. [...] Now I am ready to talk about the war. Hence I shall begin to conjure up Sarajevo for you.

Picture 1. ***The Streets***
The asphalt of Sarajevo is bloody. On the stretch from the cathedral to Planika *[shoe store]* there is not one single metre of the street that has not been bloodied. The streets are being washed, but sometimes several days pass before the traces of blood are removed. Not just once have I deduced

from the bloody stains on the marble slabs where the mortar shell fell and how the unfortunates who found themselves in the vicinity reacted. Broad smears of blood indicate that the victim, probably with leg injuries, dragged himself along trying to find shelter until the arrival of help, or else the nearest bystanders dragged the body of a dead or barely alive victim to shelter before a second bomb fell. The bravery of these people is incomprehensible, given that shells land in series of two or three, so everyone who runs to the aid of the injured risks ending up himself on the asphalt in a puddle of his own blood.

Picture 2. *The Houses*
The shattered windows dressed in thick UNPROFOR plastic sheeting, the battered frames of the windows and doors, the holes in the walls – in some places on Tito Street half of the wall is missing – façades pockmarked by shrapnel, roofs without tiles. On Radičević Street there is a demolished apartment above my grandmother's and beside my grandmother's – one mortar shell in every apartment. And eleven more apartments like that in the same row of buildings. From the outside the apartments look like caves, on the inside not even like caves: everywhere in the room there are bricks, debris, plaster, pieces of wrecked furniture, dust, shards of glass. In the Old City – Vratnik, Kovači, Baščaršija *[the Muslim bazaar]* itself are all ghostly. Every so often there is a completely demolished house, another is burned down, a third has only its walls standing – the roof and ceiling have collapsed. In the new part of town huge skyscrapers loom like charred firebrands, their cement blocks completely black and crumpled, and their steel girders twisted.

Picture 3. *The Parks*
Sarajevo, where it used to be impossible to travel twenty metres without coming upon a tree, no longer has any parks. The hills above Sarajevo, the ones, anyhow, on which there are no Chetniks, are bare. In the park by the Second Gymnasium there are scarcely any trees, the park around the Austrian house doesn't exist – there is no longer a single tree. There are no more chestnut trees on the left bank of the Miljacka, from the bridge by

the National Library almost to the Hotel National. You can see our house from the National Library, even from Bravadžiluk – there is not one solitary tree to conceal the Jajce barracks. Ćolina Kapa *[a local mountain peak]* – bare. The Great Park off Tito Street is still a park, but many of the trees have been casualties of the bombs.

The coming winter will remove even the last reminder that Sarajevo once had parks.

Picture 4. **Water**

When there is a power outage, Bačevo water station, which supplies 70% of the city with water, stops working, but even when it is working, there is very little water, so if it does manage to reach the upper storeys at all, it flows for a maximum of three-quarters of an hour to an hour. When Bačevo isn't operational (for instance, the last three weeks, with no hope of its ever starting back up again, in fact, no one even mentions it any more), all the inhabitants of the city head towards the springs on the hillsides and to the newly dug wells right downtown, towards the public fountains by the brewery and the hydrants. People haul water for kilometres by hand, and pull along on various kinds of carts or bicycles canisters, buckets, and the most diverse assortment of pots full of water. By the way, is the word "citizens" appropriate for the inhabitants of a settlement that has no public water supply, no streetlights, or any other kind of lighting, whose sewage system is just barely functioning, where public transit doesn't exist, and whose municipal government is composed of nothing but idiots? But to get back to the water. Even the water in Sarajevo is bloody. At the public fountains by the brewery a mortar shell killed eight people. I went by there immediately after the massacre. I looked at the bloody asphalt, at the bloody canisters scattered along the street, at a child's little boot in the middle of a puddle, and I asked myself if the snow that falls on the brewery will ever again be white, or will there forever, until Judgement Day, be seeping up into it bloody stains? But all the people wanted was a little water. […] Some people like to throw bombs on other people while these others are waiting their turn to draw water or buy bread. And both these ones and those are people. I still have not learned how to differentiate one from the other.

Water carts are a tale unto themselves: from market buggies and hospital stretchers, through supermarket shopping carts, airport and train-station dollies, to baby buggies fitted for the transport of water buckets and the most improbable constructions that neither could I explain nor you imagine. For example, sleds with roller-skate wheels, then bicycle wheels attached to wooden chests, then beer crates on wooden rollers. Today I saw a fellow who was carrying two canisters on either side of his bicycle handlebars, and then in a basket behind his seat three canisters, in a basket with roller-skate wheels three more canisters – that basket was very cleverly affixed to the bicycle – and, what's more, a knapsack on his back which was leaking water (I don't know how many canisters were in the knapsack, I know only that today was very cold, that it was raining, and that the guy had water pouring down his neck, his back, and his pants from his too-full knapsack).

Ilona and I have water at home. It comes almost every day for an hour or two, and as a result, we scarcely know what it's like to carry water – mind you, I carried water long enough last fall and winter from Alifakovac to Radičević Street, so I know exactly what it means to haul twenty litres of water. When the snow fell, I called into active service my old sled, and then it was, of course, much easier. This last little while Mom and Dad have taken up the habit of going for a walk from Radičević Street to the old military headquarters in front of which there is a public fountain, and they come back from their stroll with some fifty litres of water which they pull along on a small wooden children's wagon and carry in their arms.

*Picture 5. **Garbage***

The city stinks of carrion. Trash heaps every few steps. On the sidewalks, in the entranceways, in intersections and ruins, sometimes even on the roadway. Literally hills of garbage. Listen, I am not exaggerating in the least – "hills of garbage" here is not a figure of speech. Hills of garbage are hills of garbage. Real mini-landfills. The garbage is neither in bags nor in cans. It just lies scattered. In some places tenants burn refuse in bonfires from time to time, so you can always smell the stench from the smoke and see black clouds in the middle of a clear, sunny day. There are almost no heaps of garbage from which you don't see that kind of stinking smoke arising, because garbage fires can start by themselves from live embers. People cook over wood fires in 30-degree heat, because there is no alternative. As I said, there is no electricity, no gas, no oil.

Picture 6. *Dogs and Cats*

Dogs roam freely in the busiest streets of Sarajevo. Packs of them root around in the garbage heaps and rub against the legs of passers-by. Whether expensive and pedigreed or stray, all of them ragged, sickly, starved, they try to dig out of cans some remaining crumb of food. Next to a trash heap you can often find a dead litter of puppies.

Cats have not fared well in this war. There are very few of them and they look ghastly, pathetic. They fall prey to hunger or to dogs. Two of our three cats have died. One old one, Milivoj, died – maybe of old age or maybe of hunger – when at the beginning of the war we all went to Grandma's, nobody was around to feed him, not that we had anything to feed him on those occasions when we did come by to check on the house. The middle one, the tabby, starved to death because he couldn't adapt to a diet of rice and macaroni. We did try to feed him, especially after first I and then Ilona returned home, but that cat did not want to eat what we were all eating then. The greediest one has survived, but he's also pretty bedraggled.

Picture 7. *Enterocolitis*

Known in Sarajevo as "quickshititis" *[hitroseritis]*. Rare is the inhabitant of Sarajevo who hasn't had it.

Picture 8. *Jokes*

Here are a few Sarajevan jokes:
Q: What is the difference between Auschwitz and Sarajevo?
A: In Auschwitz they at least had gas.

Did you hear that Miloš *[a typically Serbian name]* has gone?
– Where to, the Chetnik s.o.b.?
To Beograd.

94

– Hah, f—— him, I always knew he was a Chetnik.

We heard from him a few days ago, he wants to come back.

– Idiot!

Mujo* is swinging in a hammock stretched across his balcony. Around him bullets are whistling. Suljo* asks him:

– Are you out of your mind, man? What are you doing?

– I'm teasing the sniper.

Here's a story that couldn't be more horrible:

A woman shouts from her window:

– Children, get out of the yard, you know there's a sniper here, you'll get shot!

A little four-year-old girl answers:

– No, we won't, daddy's sleeping.

*Picture 9. **Sarajlije** ["Sarajlije" (singular: Sarajlija) = Sarajevans]*

[...] I get around town quite a bit. I keep company with a great variety of people. From the neighbourhood unemployed to academics. I associate with cowards and with fighters from the front, with artists and policemen, and to a man, they all lampoon themselves mercilessly. Naturally, they don't miss an opportunity to skewer anyone at whom they can get a free shot. I have no intention of blathering on about the unconquerable spirit of the People – the People are sheep, and as such, interest me less than the Hungarian Sea. Nor will I bore you with talk of the spirit of Sarajevo which is indeed unique; and to speak of optimism would be the last word in idiocy. All I want to say is that the majority of these people chose to stay even though everyone had the option to leave, but none of them believes in the future of this city nor in the future of this state. But they're here all the same.

*Mujo and Suljo (= Mustafa and Suleiman), like the Irish pair Pat and Mike, are stock figures of Bosnian humour.

Picture 10. *The Softićes*

The Softićes are alive, well, and in one piece, but the death of their friends and relatives, as well as the ever greater number of cripples on the streets, reminds them at each moment that up till that moment they have enjoyed the favour of God. Thank God. One more fact: sworn atheists give thanks to God and mean it. There are few atheists left, but there are still anti-theists. But to become an anti-theist, a person first has to believe in God, and then you can go and curse His mother. If He really is great and broad-minded – He'll forgive. Anyhow, the bottom line is: this is His handiwork. The problem is that we're paying for His initial mistakes. Thanks to Him all the same, but as for His next experiment – thanks but no thanks.

I mentioned the death of relatives. Sudo Gavrankapetanović, my *[maternal]* grandfather's brother, met his end in the Chetnik prison, Kula *[= Tower]*. He was taken from his apartment in Grbavica about a year ago. […] He was eighty years old, and in the last little while, he was severely diabetic. We hope that the diabetes was the cause of his death, but it is not beyond the realm of possibility that he died from beatings or was butchered. His son Bekica said that he does not wish to receive any condolences until he sees his father's grave.

It's odd: each of us knows that stepping out into the streets of Sarajevo is playing a game with death. It's clear to each one of us that it's sheer chance that one of the 10,000 violent deaths so far in Sarajevo wasn't our own. But none of us can comprehend the death of the people close to us.

Picture 11. *Grandma*

Grandma is fine, as fine as anyone can be. She's older and weaker, ill-tempered and irascible. Of course, from time to time she forgets about all the misery surrounding her and cracks a good joke. Once, when Grandma was in the bathroom, a bomb fell in the yard behind the house and scared her witless, and, once she had "tumbled" out into the hall, she summed up the situation in her own inimitable way: "I just about ended up as a *šehit* in the john." A *šehit*, in point of fact, is a defender of the Islamic faith, though the word has acquired the additional connotation of "defender of the homeland." Well, these days, every Muslim, whether alive or killed in the war, gets the title of *šehit*. Fine, let them have it, but top honours go to Grandma for putting it all in perspective.

Epilogue

Actually, this whole letter is an epilogue to the last fifteen months. The only thing I am certain of when it comes to this war is that I wouldn't miss it for the world. Even if it costs me my life. The only thing I am certain of is that I do not want, yes, I do not want to forget even a moment of this horror. I want to remember everything. Simply so that nothing that human beings can do will ever surprise me again. I have learned a great deal. The tuition was expensive, exceedingly expensive, but it will be worth it if I come out of it alive.

Lots of love,
your Elma

15 August 1993

[a continuation of Elma's letter of 7 July to her aunt in Zagreb]

You ask how people here maintain hygiene. It's still possible to wash. Taking a shower is, for the people of Sarajevo, a fairy tale from long ago. Imagine a family of four who live on the seventeenth floor. I know them personally. Let me tell you about their washroom arrangements. The mother and father work. The children go to school. The elevator doesn't work – there's no electricity. Can they obtain enough water for all their needs? They cannot. They pass water in the toilet, and as for the other, they do it in plastic bags which they later throw onto the trash heap in front of the house. Last winter it was even worse. There probably wasn't a single apartment complex whose plumbing didn't freeze. People were scooping up shit with their Persian carpets because sewage pipes had burst and the contents from neighbours' drains were gushing out through their toilet bowls. Last winter apartment dwellers didn't dare use either their toilet bowls or their bathtubs and washstands or their kitchen sinks. They urinated into cans on their balconies and defecated into bags that went onto the trash heaps. The first days of warmer weather brought some relief because the pipes thawed, but so did the human waste gathered and well preserved during the winter. The first spring days in Sarajevo smelled of shit.

And another winter lies ahead.

THE TIMES OF LONDON, AUGUST 27, 1993

Peacekeepers face enquiry on corruption and drug claims

By Michael Evans
DEFENCE CORRESPONDENT

INVESTIGATION into

■ Sarajevo is a "sin city". The French have allegedly made use of prostitutes, and drug

they live and partly because they come from a culture where dealing on the black market is regarded as normal.

have been involved in dr smuggling. Drugs, ran from cannabis and cocain heroin are freely availabl

26 August 1993

[conclusion of the 7 July letter]

Today I went to the train station. A longing drew me. The square in front of the station is deserted. The fountain is without water. The huge windows of the station building are shattered. Out of the empty window frames peer darkness and the chill of horror. The clocks have stopped. The platforms are empty. The tracks are torn up; in some places, twisted up, they jut skywards. Here somewhere is the train bound for heaven. The railway cars are burnt, and grass has reclaimed the rail lines. There are no departures, no arrivals.

Many times I have sat on a train and taken off to Mostar for coffee. Now there are no longer any trains. No Hotel Rose and no Mostar. No locomotive whistle, no clamour of people. No people. I who have worn out my soles on hundreds of railway platforms, from the Bosnian hinterlands to the capitals of Europe, and have never been alone anywhere, whether it was two in the morning or two in the afternoon, today, this twenty-sixth day of August, Anno Domini 1993, at the height of the holiday season, I am standing alone, entirely alone, on the railway platform of my home town.

Empty train stations are horrible things.

I return to the crush of the main street. Coming to meet me is a wheel-chair. In it is a student of mine. A bomb blew off both his legs. What can I say to him? What can I say, I who used to talk to him about philosophy? I taught him logic. And as for Zoran, even if I could find the words, I can't say anything to him any more. He's dead, along with his two girlfriends.

In front of the entrance [*of the school where Elma used to be a student*], sitting on classroom chairs are two young women and an old woman in *dimije [i.e., "harem pants": traditional baggy pants worn by Muslim women]*. Two children are playing beside them, one is whining. A fourth woman comes out: in one hand she's carrying a chair, in the other, knitting. Refugees. People who have been left homeless have been sheltered in school buildings that are reasonably intact. On the third floor of my high school gapes a huge hole – at least a quarter of the classroom wall has been knocked out. Nevertheless, the building is sufficiently intact for habitation and, at the same time, for instruction.

I enter, I climb the staircase. The atmosphere is Kafkaesque: it's a school, but strange people are appearing, people who don't belong here at all. A girl with a pot full of laundry is coming down the stairs. Two little boys about ten or twelve years old go down the corridor with armfuls of wood. I come up to the staff room, but the doors are locked. A woman in a house dress, with a casserole dish covered with a dishcloth – bread, no doubt – gives me directions. I thank her and at the same moment I realize that I am not as astonished at what I have seen as I should be. Joseph K. springs to mind. At the beginning of *The Trial* he was thirty-two – as I am now. I'm no longer sure about his age, but I still know mine, I hope.

Finally a familiar school scene: two students leaning on a windowsill, notebooks in their hands, are going over a lesson. I ask if this is the staff room, and they say no, it's a German exam. I open the door slightly. In the classroom are six or seven pupils and a teacher. One student is giving an answer, the others are writing something down. It all looks like a real school during final exams. Mind you, there is no committee of three teachers, but my God – there's a war on here. I didn't look for the staff room any longer. I had seen what I wanted to see.

I want so badly to have the beginning of the next school year be the

99

beginning of peace, and to see during the next summer vacation the students leaving for their holidays on the trains which will be departing from the Sarajevo railway station. I fear, however, that we are still very far away from that.

THE NEW YORK TIMES, SEPTEMBER 30, 1993

In Lopsided Vote, Bosnia Congress Rejects Peace Plan

Continued From Page A1

amounted to a gamble that the Serbian forces will not inflict new disasters on the Muslim population, whose losses in the war are estimated to include

29 September 1993

Dear Caka,

Thanks for the magazine – it takes me back to the life I lived long ago. I don't know Italian, but that doesn't prevent me from concluding that the world is still the same – Liz still struts her stuff over three or four pages and the models are wearing fashions to take your breath away – ah! I can tell you that this news from the world from September 1993 is a consolation – for a moment at least, you get the idea that you need only take a single step to find yourself somewhere over there.

Since I don't want to spoil your mood or my own, this time I'll stick to fashion. The women of Sarajevo continue to be lovely and smartly dressed, especially the teenagers, who don't let anything cramp their style. As for the men, they're not bad either: the younger ones are heavily into the Rambo look *[fatigues, bandannas, etc.]*, and, so help me God, so are a few of the older ones. All of them are wearing ponytails, and not because the barbershops have closed – many have resolved not to cut their hair until the war is over. And therefore it's not unusual to meet middle-aged (or a little more than middle-aged) gentlemen in dark suits and impeccably white shirts with the obligatory neatly knotted ties and the inevitable briefcases and perfectly groomed hair – tied in a ponytail. Surreal, in accordance with our present circumstances. Nevertheless, what amazes me the most is the whiteness of the blouses, shirts, T-shirts, pants, and so on – and they're all *ironed.* I'm always wondering – how? given everything that there isn't: electricity, water, gas, blah, blah, blah. You probably know what all is "in short supply" here (how do you like that for a euphemism? [...] But nevertheless, I myself am "that way," too, I mean, clean and "pressed."

It's now 9:15 p.m. I'm sitting in the kitchen on the top floor of our house on Alifakovac. [...] When I cast a glance to the left, barely visible on the wall in the darkness is the gleam of a vast array of kitchen necessities hanging from nails: a colander, a strainer, large spoons, forks, tongs for pastries (ah, pastries – in what blessed period of humanity did people eat pastries?), and sundry other spoon-shaped, fork-shaped, reticulated and prehensile instruments which my mother (and my father with undiminished enthusiasm) bought and whose purpose I don't know. Directly underneath is a work surface *[a tabletop used as a counter]* full of dirty dishes – I'm hopeless at housekeeping even when there is running water, and Ilona is even worse. (I must say, nonetheless, that I'm not a bad cook – cooking as a creative task is for me a challenge, especially now, when the selection of foodstuffs at the market – that I can afford – is nil.)

But let me continue with my stylistic composition, "A Description of My Kitchen." Below this work table with the dirty dishes are food bowls for our cat. A black tom by the name of Vasko has been curled up on the couch since the beginning of this narrative.

Why am I writing to you about my kitchen? You're dear to me and I want somehow to give you a picture of *me*, instead of just philosophizing a lot about life, war, love, etc., etc. I'll tell you only that I'm enjoying being in this kitchen in this moment. And I'll tell you too that there was a time when I couldn't even imagine reading, writing, or engaging in any kind of intellectual discipline amid dirty dishes and leftovers from dinner ("leftovers" is purely a figure of speech – we had perfect spaghetti with even more perfect sauce and none of it was left over, as indeed, for the last eighteen months there has never been anything left on a plate except when it was being saved for the next day). Anyhow, I was saying that Elma the intellectual used to be incapable of working in prosaic kitchen conditions – for work I needed my (and Ilona's) bedroom, my desk, my books with their serious titles and the like – I must have been infinitely tiresome.

101

I'll ask you now to look over on my right side – there is the most appealing object in my kitchen: the window. A window in the front of the house, right under the roof. From it you can see the whole of Sedrenik, Vratnik, Mejtaš, Bjelave, Breka, Ciglane, and further down to the UNIS skyscrapers *[the two highest in Sarajevo, the pair were popularly nick-named Momo (a Serbian name) and Uzeir (Muslim); both have been badly damaged.]* You can get a glimpse of Grbavica (which is to say: I can see across the border) *[Grbavica was then under Bosnian Serb control]*. The scene spread out before me at this moment is magical: as far as the eye can see, there is not a single light, but as a result the city is bathed in sil-very moonlight. It is so light out that I can see the windows on the white façades of some houses, and it seems to me that I could count the minarets of as many mosques now at 11:15 p.m. as I could today at 11:15 a.m. This, besides being romantic, is also comforting, because today, after two months, shelling of the city started up again – only half an hour after the radio announced the results of the vote in Parliament for or against the peace plan.* (The decision was for the peace plan, but only on condi-tion that the other side withdraw from forcibly seized territories, which is a first-class piece of bafflegab, because, if they hadn't seized the territories, and forcibly at that – I've never heard of anyone seizing anything ami-cably – there wouldn't be any reason for them to be voting for or against the "peace" (oh, right) plan.) So anyhow, just half an hour after the news announcement (more precisely, twenty minutes after) five bombs fell. Can you guess where? In Vaso Miskin Street right on the corner by the Planika shoe store, on the roof of the Market building, two in the park near Svjetlost publishers, and one in Radojko Lokić Street. It looks as though only one boy was injured – I say "only" because it was 3:20 p.m. and the streets were full of people. Thanks to the fact that the first bomb fell on the roof of the Market and the already well-drilled Sarajevans had enough time (about two minutes or even a little less) to take cover, there weren't more future invalids or former people.

There, I've done it, I've started on the war again. You see how hard it

*The Owen-Stoltenberg proposal for the partition of BiH.

is even for me, who used to spend hours, days, months, lost in the recesses of my own imagination, to escape the reality of the misery in which we are living – or, more accurately, perishing.

I won't pursue that theme. All the same I'm still capable of sending what we call reality to the devil, at least for a few hours at night, and to write about the silver gleam on the minarets of the mosques of Sarajevo and about the gloriously beautiful nights without electricity. One day, when this city turns into a City once again, I personally, as sovereign of its most beautiful nights, will extinguish all its lights and decree compulsory moonlight tours for all domestic and foreign tourists, for all former, current, and future lovers.

It looks as though it really is time for me to end this scribbling. [...] I've lit a new candle, and Ilona will throttle me tomorrow because candles are more precious than gold. Besides, I'm out of paper.

All the best from your best friend Elma.

4 November 1993

Dear Caka,
Winter has begun, and so we can no longer make use of our large improvised Arborite kitchen. We have no heat. Improvisation is again the order of the day: we live in the smallest room in our house, which used to be my parents' bedroom, and which was always stuffed to bursting with furniture (whatever couldn't find a place somewhere else ended up here); it was the most cluttered and least visited space. Now my sister, my cousin – a refugee from Mostar who came to us two weeks ago – and I live in it. We have, of course, fixed it up. Now there are two beds, one small end table, two low shelves, one small dining-room table, and a little wood stove which is supposed to keep us from freezing this winter. On this little stove, which looks as though it came out of a children's storybook, is a large pot with my laundry in it – I've been soaking it for three days now – and a pot of peas – that was our lunch today and that will be our lunch tomorrow (I don't need to remind you that it contains neither smoked ribs nor any other kind of meat) – and a teapot with water that is already almost cold. The

stove is cold because there is just enough fuel to cook lunch, but not enough for a luxury like letter writing. And of course the room is cold, too. I'm wearing a cotton undershirt, pyjamas, a track suit, a thick woollen dress, thick woollen socks (torn, mind you). My cousin Yasmina is sitting wrapped in a blanket reading *[author Danilo]* Kiš; Ilona is sleeping in a sleeping bag. A sleeping bag is a wonderful thing: it's warm, and on top of that, it saves on bed linen, seeing as – you know the refrain already – there's no water, there's no electricity, there's no gas.

In the days before the war, whenever I would sit down to write, I liked to have beside me a teapot of good Indian tea, strong, boiling hot, unsweetened (sometimes I would add two or three drops of condensed milk), or else a *džezva [a Turkish coffee pot]* of equally hot, strong, and bitter coffee. Tonight I'm sipping barely lukewarm water from that teapot, because we've already drunk our daily quota of tea made from quince leaves, gathered, with the kind forbearance of our neighbours, from the garden next door; and we won't be heating the stove up again until tomorrow afternoon. I'm down to the last cigarettes from the last pack I have and I don't know when I'll be able to treat myself to another.

Since yesterday all you can get at the market is the sort of stuff you used to get there before the war – things like cabbages, potatoes, onions, leeks, etc. – but at fantastically high prices in Deutschmarks. The police have chased off the black marketeers who used to sell everything: from chewing gum out of American lunch-packs, to meat (an abstract noun for 90% of the inhabitants of Sarajevo) and the finest Swiss chocolates to the best Scotch whiskies, French cognacs, German beers, and even auto parts and astrakhan fur coats, so that I could almost believe that the government had finally picked itself up after a knockout punch (even now the stubbornest people continue to hope that it wasn't a knockout). Well, that's enough about the government, for I don't intend to talk politics even though that is, next to sprinting across intersections, the favourite sport here.

Just one more note on the black market: we bought our sweet little stove, well, half of it, with the proceeds from the sale of a pound of Vegeta *[soup mix]* that we had been saving for a year for just such a God-forbid-we-should-need-to occasion and a hundred-gram jar of Nescafé *[instant coffee]* which Ilona had got from some journalist, and which we, once again, had saved for a special occasion, à la birthday, New Year's Eve, or (silly us) the end of the war. I must confess that, as far as I'm concerned, the "rule of law" came along a bit too soon. After all, I still have half a kilo of Vegeta and a kilo of coffee – God bless the friend who brought it – but no wood. As you can see, I was supposed to exchange the spices and the coffee for fuel. You know what the funniest part of all this is? Not long ago we got a package from Seka with … another half kilo of the famous Vegeta and a kilo of coffee! We could be having a bath in that divine black beverage and rinsing in delicately spiced broth, if only we had something to cook them with. And to make the absurd still more absurd, consider the following fact: months before we came into this wealth of coffee, I didn't have the slightest chance, in my very own home, of being able to "splurge" and toss back even a thimbleful.

This letter is considerably different in tone from my last one. If you think it's my last gasp, a desperate scream of "Help!"*, you're wrong. I was given to depression, melancholy, and related pathologies in the good old days when there wasn't nearly as much cause for it as there has been in the past two years. I'm just trying to describe to you the present situation here in this most remote corner of the universe.

All in all, I really have no right to complain – I'm alive and well and I'm still not starving, all the members of my household are also fine. Even my grandmother, who is eighty-seven years old, is functioning perfectly well (given her years and the circumstances in which she's living them out). My parents are living with her and only they have an adequate conception of her unbelievable vitality.

Caka, I'm dreadfully tired and I'll continue this tomorrow. This is just one more proof that I too am aging – there was a time when I could be at the typewriter all night and the whole next day, not stopping for as long as I had anything to say, but alas!, it looks as though those days are over.

Here's one of the local jokes:

You know how a smart Bosnian talks to a stupid one?

*"Help!" is in English in the original.

– By satellite.

Not bad, eh?

– Suljo's in heaven, Mujo's in hell. They get an urge to talk to their families in Sarajevo. Suljo calls from heaven, talks for half an hour, and gets charged $200. Mujo phones from hell, talks for half an hour, and it costs him twenty cents. Suljo's pissed off, so he goes to the phone company and says, "Look, how is this possible? I call Sarajevo from heaven, talk for half an hour, and pay two hundred dollars. Mujo calls Sarajevo from hell, talks for half an hour, and pays only twenty cents!"

The employee at the wicket replies, "Well, Mr. Suljo, your call was long distance, but Mujo's was a local call."

As you can see, Sarajevo still resembles, at least a little bit, that other Sarajevo. Here we still respond to bitterness and horror with jokes – bitter, dirty, defiant ones. And it's precisely on account of that spirit that I can't make my peace with the fact that we allowed stupidity to tailor our fate. Some smart person once said: If stupidity hurt, people would be screaming to high heaven. This person got only one thing wrong: the conditional. For here, stupidity in truth does hurt, and people really are screaming, to heaven and even higher. The problem is that the ones they're crying out to are deaf. Albert Camus says, "There is no fate that can't be surmounted with scorn." Old Camus was right in that, as he was in everything he said, but that intelligent thought gives me no comfort, nor does any other intelligent thought, whether his or anyone else's. Scorn is non-action, and I am not ready for non-action, not yet.

Each of these timeless truths from the geniuses that have trodden our dear Mother Earth offers me one thing only: sobering clarity. Not one of them offers me comfort. And that's why, Caka, once I get my hands on a certain quantity of that blessed vice, His Majesty Alcohol, I'm going to get so drunk that I won't sober up for the rest of my life, for it's better to be drunk on hooch than on ideas and quasi-ideas, ideologies and sub-ideologies *[ideja i idejica, ideologija i ideologijica – Elma expresses her scorn with diminutives]*.

In the meantime, it's necessary to persevere through this s(h)it-uation, because it will be impossible otherwise to get to those certain quantities of the aforementioned liquid. You can't get it here, or rather, you can, but at ridiculous prices – and there's no sense buying it instead of firewood, since that would mean freezing to death in very short order, and we poor human beings do need to enjoy some creature comforts as well. That's my opinion, anyhow.

Well, seeing as how I'm still rambling on, I've come to the conclusion that I'm not yet "for the trash heap." My love of writing is stronger than my love for the god Morpheus. It's true that his realm is the securest refuge for weary souls, but my soul, it seems, is not too exhausted. On the other hand, my light is dying – the candle is going out. Therefore – until tomorrow. Good night....

6 November 1993

[a continuation of the 4 November letter to Caka]
Today we celebrated my mother's birthday. [...] Considering that there were five of us, the meal was not all that abundant, but for our shrunken stomachs it was completely satisfactory. There was also dessert. I assume that somewhere in the cruel and hostile world, they are still making rich cakes with a full complement of eggs, walnuts, chocolate, raisins, candied fruit, rum, etc., etc., though frankly, I'm no longer the slightest bit certain that I know what all those divine items are actually for, because, believe me, pastries are perfectly good even without them. Here's a recipe for a wartime dessert called "Chocolate":
–   5 fildžans* of powdered milk
–   1 fildžan cocoa
Mix well.

In a separate bowl (pot) put:
–   1 fildžan cooking oil
–   1 fildžan water and
–   5 !!! fildžans sugar (which is actually an enormous amount of sweetener for our situation – the last sugar we got from humanitarian

---

*fildžan = a small cup without a handle used for Turkish coffee.

aid was a month and eighteen days ago, 250 grams per person)

Simmer the three aforementioned ingredients over low heat, stirring constantly, and then pour this sauce over the milk and cocoa mixture. Pour the resulting mixture into a suitable baking pan, smooth it a little, and then wait for it to cool. Cut it into squares and eat it [...] quickly, so you don't find yourself in the position of having a sudden explosion in the vicinity of your little garden of gastronomical pleasure drive a sweet mouthful into your windpipe, thus ending your precious young life in an exceptionally unheroic fashion. Just imagine the wording of the obituary: "She was killed by a traitorous morsel at the moment of the aggressor's shelling."

But when I speak of food, I can't not mention the queues of hungry people who wait patiently for hours for one of the humanitarian organizations to distribute some soup or a handful of rice, some mashed potatoes. I have to write about them [...] for the sake of the pangs of conscience that I feel – which are totally irrational, since I am not taking food away from anybody, I'm not stealing, I'm not a war profiteer, but nevertheless, I am full, and they are hungry.

I pass by one of those hungry queues every day as I return home from work, usually between four and five in the afternoon. [...] I make a point of passing by as quickly as possible and of not letting my glance settle on any of them. I'm embarrassed because I think they're embarrassed, though that is in fact disgusting hypocrisy, for undoubtedly I am thinking that I would find it horrible to have to stand and put out my hand for a little food. But what is indecent about the desire to survive?

The faces of the people waiting are exhausted, their eyes restless, their whole body ready to react to the signal that the food has arrived or to anyone's attempt to jump queue. In their hands they hold pots, plastic bowls, the packaging from long-forgotten sweets, army ration kits, and even the most ordinary plastic bags.

People stand quietly until the food arrives, and then begin the shoving, the bickering, and often, the shouting matches. The food is brought in large cauldrons that are set down directly on the pavement, and it is passed out by a young woman – one serving per person from a large ladle like the kind used in dormitory dining halls. It can happen that not everyone who was waiting for a meal gets it. Yesterday I saw a woman kneeling on the street and scraping the empty cauldron with her spoon, trying to collect the last particles of food. Everyone else stood there, not moving, not saying anything. Her scraping was so feverish, her hunger so ravenous that no one could come up with any reproach, no harsh word or customary profanity was heard, no impatient shout.

The people who stand in this queue for food in the street are in no way distinguishable from the people who stand in such queues in the public kitchens, and nowadays in Sarajevo anyone who can get food in one of these kitchens has won the jackpot. Truly rare are the lucky ones who have this privilege at their place of work. All of us, in point of fact, stand in some food queue or other, the only difference being that standing in the street leaves you more exposed to the curiosity of others.

Listen, before we make a date for a cappuccino and apple strudel (nice and flaky, with cinnamon sprinkled on top and lots of icing sugar, still warm – taken from the oven about half an hour earlier and left at room temperature) at the Esplanade about five o'clock (in the afternoon, obviously), I'll have to beg you to wait for me a minute or two in case I'm late – you know how it is, it's November, and you can't be sure about Sarajevo airport even in the middle of summer.

9 December 1993

[a continuation of the 4 November letter to Caka]
In all this time, I have not had the opportunity to finish this letter. For the days are short, and I've had just barely enough candles to allow me, upon returning from work, to make dinner, to eat it, and then – straight to bed. It feels silly to us to go to bed at a quarter past seven in the evening, so we have taken up the practice of "deep meditations" in total darkness. They end with a tour of sleep duty that lasts until about 10 p.m., when we awake – usually reluctantly – and with laborious effort drag ourselves out from under the warm blankets; and, thus warmed up, we would make our beds in the cold bedroom and snuggle up in the ice-cold bedding. And so we pay off the debt of the endless wartime nights of Sarajevo. But during

the daytime I don't have time to write, and anyway I wouldn't know how. Night-time is when I'm at peace, the time when my being slips free of the cruel strictures of impeccable daytime functioning and when my brain disentangles itself from the tight weave of precise reasoning and planning and floats into the freedom of fluid imaginings and memories.

In point of fact, things have somewhat improved recently in Sarajevo with regard to electricity, which is to say, we occasionally have some, but not in all areas of the city; and I happen to live in one of the areas to which electricity has not "paid a visit" for a full seven months. This, however, has its good side: it spares me heavy work on the night shift (unpaid, of course). Because when in the night, suddenly, the chandeliers light up in the homes of Sarajevo, the city goes on red alert. Everyone leaps out of bed; on go the stoves, the vacuum cleaners, and even the washing machines; and the drowsy inhabitants of this city that is not a city fling themselves into nocturnal orgies of … housework. The vacuum cleaners roar, laundry is done – manually and by machine (because there is no water most of the time, water is poured carefully – by hand – from cans into the washing machines: this is what we call "the semi-automatic wash cycle"); a few days' supply of bread is baked, the mounds of laundry that have accumulated over the time (say, three to four months) when nary a "drop" of electricity reached the city are ironed. Whoever is lucky enough to have kept some water in their hot-water tank switches that on as well, in the hopes that one fine day they will be able even to have a shower – if they are willing, that is, to risk having precious water drain out of their bathtub. And so it goes the whole night, or at least, as long as the electrons grace the homes with their presence. In the morning people show up at work pale, with bags under their eyes, but almost happy. Just today I overheard a conversation between two of my male co-workers (whose wives and children have left Sarajevo), and it went like this:

– Last night I got a lot done: I washed, I vacuum-cleaned.…

– I had electricity at my place too. I ironed from three to seven this morning*.

*The full humour of this conversation cannot be conveyed in English. The men use feminine forms (*prala*, *usisavala*, *peglala*) – speaking, as it were, in a kind of grammatical falsetto.

This may appear charming, perhaps it may seem to you that things in Sarajevo are getting easier, but that is a cruel deception. People struggle with all their might to maintain some kind of normal day-to-day life, to see that their homes are tidy, that their clothes are clean and pressed, but these details, once so ordinary, now consume their whole days and nights, all their strength and inventiveness and competence. When I start to reflect on this wretched life of ours here, all my thoughts pale by comparison with one image that dogs me mercilessly: the circus. Behind the dazzle of the circus ring, a small zoo. You pay admission to see the animals that perform in the program. The elephant. A magnificent colossus. His left fore-leg and his right hind leg bound with short chains attached to thick iron pegs stuck in the ground. He can't go anywhere. But he moves. Uniformly, in an improbably slow rhythm, his head and trunk turn sluggishly: left, right, left …; just so, his free legs, front and back, alternate: left, right, left, right.… Caka, I stood and watched and choked on my tears of grief and helplessness. I stood in front of that majestic animal and wept, yes, wept, seeing him so reduced. I don't remember how long the intermission last-ed, I know only that I spent the whole time standing in front of that ele-phant and that he spent the whole time repeating the same movements: left, right, left, right, left.… I went to that circus show one more time and everything was the same. That elephant – is Sarajevo. Through sheer iner-tia, people continue to do the same things they used to do in peacetime, things that in these present circumstances have utterly lost their meaning. Left, right, left … with no sense to it at all – that is life in Sarajevo.

Today I was sitting in a little café across the street from the department store, right next to the *Dubrovnik* cinema – you remember, Caka – there was always some snackbar or other there. These days there's a flower shop and a café there. All glass, lots of flowers – fake ones. Instead of fresh roses, irises, lilies, gladioli, carnations, orchids, are artificial flow-ers, standing in large vases. And people are coming and buying them. The florist selects flowers and arranges them. He wraps them in tissue paper and cellophane and ties them with a bow. From time to time one of the young men carries off lovely large bouquets to some Sarajevo address. In Sarajevo there are no fresh flowers – in December there's no chance of

111

picking any from a garden or park, and even if they could be sent from the greenhouses in Herzegovina, they couldn't be brought into the city. It's sad. A city without flowers.

One day recently I was invited to a wedding. A familiar scene, everything as it should be – the white wedding gown and the dark suit, the veil and the bow-tie. The bride, carrying a bridal bouquet of white linen roses, entered the wedding hall pale and a little frightened, and after her ten or so friends, all of them dressed to the nines and in fine form, with huge bouquets of artificial flowers in various colours. Those flowers left a grotesque impression upon me. I couldn't rid myself of the feeling that I was at a funeral, because the bouquets reminded me of those horrible plastic funeral wreaths. It was as though Death were sitting there in the hall among us. The only question was whom had he chosen as his first sweetheart.

I've come a long way from the café. I wanted to describe to you its atmosphere, which is, admittedly, a little kitschy because of those ever-present artificial flowers, but is nevertheless not unpleasant – the golden oldies music and the generally urbane faces of the clientele. There are even some pastries: made according to wartime recipes, it goes without saying, but they slide down our undiscerning gullets, long unused to such delicacies, like real jellyrolls or rumballs (though they're without rum, naturally). Prices are in Deutschmarks. Actually, you could pay in Bosnian state coupons, except that it would take me approximately a month and a half to earn the price of one coffee. As it turned out, I was treated to the coffee and pastry and it felt really good, so much so that I almost forgot that ugly taste of pennilessness, the feeling that you just do not have the money to pay for one fucking coffee, let alone to treat someone else. Anyhow, what I in fact wanted to tell you was that people are sitting in bars, coffee shops and restaurants. That they're going to the movies and the theatre, that concerts, exhibitions, children's shows are being organized – but what of it? How am I to go when afterwards, returning home, I'll trip fifteen times and hit the asphalt five times, as I grope my way home through the thick darkness, through the mud, the garbage, and the packs of dogs that roam the streets or rummage through the trash heaps looking for some morsel for themselves?

While we're on the subject of trash heaps: it's not just the dogs that rummage around in them. People also pick through the cans, looking for food, cigarette butts, or packaging suitable for fuel. You'll come across them most often in the morning, from dawn until nine or ten (the time when they go to their homes to prepare lunch). And now that I mention cigarettes: a number of times already I've come across a tall blonde young woman, well-dressed, carefully picking butts out of the refuse and placing them in a little cardboard box. And today an older woman who was walking beside me stopped for a moment, bent over quickly and picked up from the street a half-smoked cigarette, hurriedly shoved it into her coat pocket, threw me a sidelong glance, and quickened her pace.

Caka, I'm sick to my soul. I used to think that soul-sickness was just a metaphor, but it's not. Something inside me is hurting, Caka, squeezing me. I feel a tightness inside, the tension of the urge to do something, but I'm helpless. All I can do is scream, and I'm not even doing that.

And yet, I wouldn't miss this war for anything in the world. Not for any life in peace and happiness and prosperity would I exchange this experience of misery and death. Don't ask me why. It's simply the way I am: bloodyminded. There is in me a kind of spite that I myself am not clear about. The war has become my lifestyle. I wonder when I'll feel like changing my style, but what scares me the most is the answer to the question, will I know how to change it?

Nevertheless, I have resolved that we will survive, I and those dearest to me. There are so many things that I have neglected to do because of my laziness, and I cannot allow myself to be killed. If for no other reason than for these letters. There is no chance that I'll have a "change of address" before I write down everything that I have to say. [...] I have to confess that I have had doubts for a long time about even trying to speak about this war to people who haven't lived it themselves. And not because it would be impossible to describe it, but because any war in which we ourselves are not involved is always pushed to the margins to make room for our private everyday "wars" which, though they may not be bloody, are nevertheless laborious struggles to realize our dreams (and we know how painful it can be to transform dreams into reality). I still think that personal

113

experience is difficult to communicate to others, but the sympathy and desire on the part of people I don't know who live in some happier galaxy to help one of the many prisoners of the unreason and human stupidity which is, I am deeply convinced, innate to human beings, and not just to some people or to some nations (the problem is purely our "Wild West" nature – who will draw first), have so put me to shame that I feel both the need and the duty to send "reports" from Sarajevo which are, admittedly, far from good journalism, but lo and behold, they obviously possess some power to elicit goodness which is – oh, the absurdity – also characteristic of this unfortunate species of ours.

The city is being shelled again. The bombs are falling somewhere close by, the windows are rattling and the walls are shaking. I have a knot in my stomach, and my heart is pounding frantically. […] I don't know, Caka, I don't know. It's not my custom to be afraid, nor to have a tingling sensation flowing in a tide from my stomach to my larynx, but there you have it, these last few days…. I don't know, and it's not even important, after all: "Mujo has endured worse." And he'll endure the very worst and the worse than very worst. So….

It's time for me to finish writing. I'm cold and yes, I'm afraid. Some devil has entered my bones. I'm going to sleep this off – I'm lucky that I still can sleep like a baby, even if everything were to come crashing down around me.

Lots of love, lots!

16 December 1993

[a continuation of her letter to Caka]

Fuck, the minute I even think that in some book of world history some asshole is going to write about this war as a conflict of national and religious interests between ethnic groups located in the perpetually unstable region of the Balkans, which lasted from 1991 to whenever, I could just blow this whole planet to bits so that not a particle of it remains.

Meanwhile, here there is terror, blood, and death. […] There isn't a square inch of pavement in Sarajevo that hasn't had blood spilled on it.

Can you believe it – the rain came down all that afternoon, the whole night and the next morning, and it still didn't wash away the blood of the unfortunates who died *hungry*, for in this town everyone is hungry, *dirty*, for in this town water is measured out in coffee spoons, and *terrified*, for there isn't a person on these streets whose sweat doesn't smell of fear. Puddles of blood have collected in the holes made by shrapnel and in the dust from the façades and bricks turned to powder by the bombs. It's not the first time I've walked through human blood – that's a normal thing in Sarajevo – but I can't fathom how much blood there must have been for it not to have been washed away by the rain.

THE GLOBE AND MAIL, DECEMBER 29, 1993

Words often only UN weapon

Starved for funds amid more calls for help, peacekeepers soldier on

BY GERALDINE BROOKS
The Wall Street Journal
United Nations

One recent morning, the meeting started with discussion of

times. Angola will join a queue with all other UN peacekeeping

When peacekeeping missions grow, the world peers scorn-

29 December 1993

Dear Dunja,

Do you know how bright moonlit nights are in a city covered in snow? […] Right now it's early morning – four hours after midnight, and at least two and a half hours before dawn. The curtains on the window in our bedroom are drawn back, and a silvery light is pouring into the room. The contours of every object are clearly visible and everything has taken on a mystical appearance. And when you look through the window the view is unreal. Our yard is shining. The cherry tree, snow on its branches, is sparkling; it seems to me that enclosed within it is a whole little world full of wonders, beauties, and tales. A little closer to me is a dark old pear tree, with a knotty trunk and crooked branches: with its tiny branches bent under frozen snow against the backdrop of a pale sky, it looks unearthly. Everything is strange, everything is silver, everything is peaceful. And the moon is enormous, brilliant, magnificent. Everything is full of whispers, of some secret, invisible life.

And all this "thanks to" the war – if it weren't for the war even at this soundless hour one of the windows of the neighbouring houses would be lit up, and the streetlight would dim and scatter that lustrous silver.

Are you wondering why I'm awake at this hour? The answer is quite simple: yesterday Ilona and I lay down right after supper, and that was about 5 p.m., to rest a little after a hard day. We hadn't gone to work, but on account of that we'd cleaned house, done the laundry (by hand in ice-cold water, naturally), split firewood, made some minor repairs à la replacing tiles after the hurricane winds of the last few days, fixing our wood stove, attempting to get our sink in working order – it had evidently got fed up with everything and started to leak water on all sides – doing the dishes and making dinner. Well, anyhow, not to prolong this enumeration of trivialities which under these circumstances cease to be trivial and become existential problems, let me just say that we ate dinner and agreed that it was time to rest our bodies and souls and to save on candles for at least two hours. You know what happened: we woke up at ten in the evening, changed into our pyjamas, and went beddy-byes. That's the daily – or, in this case, nightly – routine in Sarajevo. To think that there existed a time when at that hour I would be going into my first café of that evening, or else sitting down at my desk surrounded by a pile of books, full of drive and enthusiasm to learn or write something new. I haven't read anything for ages, because reading at night by candle- or lamplight represents a considerable strain, as my eyesight has deteriorated and I'd need to get reading glasses (geriatric farsightedness, ha! ha!), but frames were pretty expensive even in the best of times, and nowadays they haven't gotten any cheaper, while everything else has become frightfully expensive. I miss reading terribly. I'm getting stupid and I'm beginning to forget the rudimentary facts in my own field. It sometimes happens that I can't recall the name of some important philosopher (my degree was in philosophy and literature) or elementary definitions in formal logic (I taught it for two years in a high school). Dreadful!

Yesterday my good friend Dragan and I went to see our mutual friend. High school buddies. Dragan is a painter, Haris is an electrical engineer. We were in the same grade and have stayed friends to the present day. Haris

116

lives on Obala Street, near the *[Gavrilo]* Princip Bridge. On the third floor. His apartment faces Mt. Trebević. A location like that in Sarajevo is a synonym for terror. From Trebević come mortar shells and snipers' bullets. Our friend is waiting for us, he lets us in his large kitchen.

We converse. About ordinary things. Work, water, electricity, gas, negotiations. Wartime conversations. Letters. Haris got a letter from his wife and children. They are in Sweden. Refugees. Their letters are full of sadness and homesickness. He reads us an excerpt. They're fine. They're well set up. They have a tiny apartment in a house on the shore of some lake or some fjord, I'm not sure any more. The kids are going to school. They're good students. Their days are filled with a variety of activities, they go to music and dance lessons. The scenery there is spectacular, but it's cold and it's somehow, somehow different. The people are pleasant, but only pleasant. Frankly, the Swedes are putting up with them. His wife is lonely. She doesn't yet have a work permit. She hasn't made any friends, and she doesn't think she will ever be able to establish any close connections either with Bosnians there or with the Swedes. She's having a hard time. She's homesick for Sarajevo, she misses her husband. All the worries and problems that she used to share with Haris have now fallen on her shoulders alone. And so when she does relax a little, when her mood lifts a bit, she suffers because she is not with him. She wants to come back. Despite the war, the misery and the death. "I can't explain it to you, my love, everyone here is good to us. We're not hungry and we're warm. But, darling, my life is not here."

Dragan's wife and son are in France. Staying with some relatives. And he gets similar letters. What are they to do? The two of them talk. I'm a fifth wheel here. I have no family of my own, and my parents and sister are here. I listen to them. Should they stay in this city or leave? Leave for where? How? They were born here. Grew up, went to school here. Their friends are here. This is their city. This is where they left from to go travelling and this is where they came back to. Everything that they've built, they've built here. They're still young. It's not too late for them to start over in some more fortunate spot on this planet. But must they flee? Will there be an end to this war, and how will things be afterwards? To leave now almost certainly means to leave for good.

No one asks whether he will survive. That question is taken for granted in Sarajevo. And the answer is: maybe, but then again, maybe not. Not even the awareness that you're alive only by chance is a sufficiently strong argument for the decision to leave here.

It's already seven, time for me to start going about the customary kitchen tasks – stoking the stove, baking the *maslenice [unleavened pastry dough, like a pie crust]*, preparing breakfast, getting ready for work, etc. Now it occurs to me that all these tasks will sound so straightforward, but here all this is full of complications.

I'll probably continue this letter next year – it's important to celebrate New Year's here, too, if for no other reason than in order not to lose any of our fine customs, since we're finding it difficult to free ourselves of our bad ones.

2 J a n u a r y 1 9 9 4

[a continuation of the 29 December letter to Dunja]

New Year's Eve. I celebrated it with friends in an apartment on the top (eleventh) floor of a building right in the centre of town. I left home a little before six o'clock, full of fear because immediately before that, three mortar shells had landed somewhere very near. I came down the hill near home feeling my way through the murky darkness on thin ice like finest glass – the day had been unusually warm, so the snow had melted and then frozen solid in the evening. I breathed a sigh of relief when I found myself on level ground, and set off, still cautiously, but much more quickly over the bridge. The first sinister omen that evening was the ruins of the National Library, whose outlines were beginning to detach themselves from the surrounding darkness. Even in the gloom it was apparent that that magnificent building had been reduced to rubble. Instead of windows there were gaping holes; I caught glimpses of the broken stone of the marble steps. Suddenly the headlights of a stray automobile gliding past me like a phantom lit up those dreadful remains, and the full horror of the ruins bore in upon me – some beams which had fallen from nowhere, masonry and bricks from a collapsed ceiling, the skeletons of iron book-shelves, some wires – Dunja, I didn't feel terror, I felt the death of an abandoned world. The car passed by, the light from the headlights disap-peared, and I stopped. I watched the darkness thickening in the openings in which there once stood doors and I tried to find within myself some feeling which would push me to tears: love for that place where I spent my student days, nostalgia for the past which had been so beautiful. I tried to recollect the faces of the colleagues I had met there and the librarians who had lent me books; I wanted to recall the smell of the reading room and the colours of the painted ceilings. Nothing – as though nothing of that had ever existed. Finally I tried to hate the people who had done this, but I couldn't. Dunja, I was dead. There was more pain and more love in the marble of the ruined columns than there was in me.

I continued on my way. Cold and empty and old. I followed the street-car tracks. I kept my eyes on the asphalt in front of me, though I knew that I was passing by completely destroyed old Bosnian houses and that soon I would pass by a house whose metal roof has been hanging, almost touch-ing the street, for a whole year now, and swinging in even the gentlest breeze, threatening to turn someday into a guillotine. Oh yes, these pictures of the horror of Sarajevo have surfaced unbidden and have remained in my consciousness, more powerful than any desire I might have to erase them.

I encountered my first passer-by near the old Orthodox church. The mystical atmosphere of that building has always enticed me to enter and to breathe in the smell of incense and humid stone, to light a candle, one for the dead and another for the living (I had always lit candles for all the dead and all the living of this world). That little church has been terribly damaged – the mortars that come from the hills don't distinguish between mosque and church, human and animal, they kill everything with a glim-mer of life within it and destroy everything that bears the seal of human loveliness. But mortars don't fire themselves – I ask myself, what differ-entiates the killer from the victim? What defines the difference between the one who hasn't yet succeeded in killing me and me who as yet haven't tried to kill him? Only these conditional sentences: "If I had taken better aim, I would have killed her," and "If I get the chance, I'll kill him."

At that old church, the second stage of my journey began. Now memories and feelings started to wash over me in waves. I recalled my friend Maja, a pair of Englishmen, David and Philip, and a first officer of some transatlantic ship. Of the Englishmen who had come to Sarajevo, one was Maja's friend, and the other the friend of the friend. The two of us took them on a tour of the city, and here, in front of the church, the first officer joined us, without invitation and without questions. To which happy nation he belonged, I have no idea. I wouldn't say he was a Briton – we were all speaking English, but his, like mine, wasn't exactly English. [...] He wasn't interested in sightseeing, he was alone and needed company. He was so insistent about stopping for a drink that in the end we gave up on history and holed ourselves up in the coolness of a tavern. And the officer ordered rounds of drinks, and the full glasses lined themselves in front of us with incredible speed. We kept looking at each other because our Maecenas [= *our benefactor, our patron*] was pouring himself cognac as if out of an empty bottle. The talk was like pouring from one sieve to another. All I remember was that this guy had been married five times, and engaged eleven times altogether, and, insofar as I could understand, at the time of our encounter he was not even engaged. He had come to Sarajevo just like that, for something to do – he was on vacation. He allowed us to crawl stiffly out of the tavern only when it was already time for him to go back to the hotel, pick up his things, have dinner somewhere and get on a train to Zagreb so he could catch the first plane to Frankfurt – he was going to some soccer tournament. The waiter was overjoyed because we left behind us a half gallon of untouched cognac and the single empty glass out of which our officer had already downed gallons.

The next memory was of a scene with umbrellas. Across from the old Sephardic synagogue, and a little farther down in a low house, was an umbrella repair shop. Rain was pouring down in buckets, and my friend (with whom I was hopelessly in love) and I (with whom he was hopelessly not in love) were trying to take cover under my raincoat, which was the most delicate shade of pink. At the same time, out from the umbrella repair shop steps a man with at least five "brollies." He stands in the rain and can't seem to find what must be his most treasured possession. He's standing there, getting soaked, checking everywhere, turning this way and that, looking around, while rivulets pour off him. He goes back into the shop. The two of us, as daft as he is, stand there, splitting our sides laughing, and we wait to see how the story will end. The man comes back out, visibly frustrated, with yet another umbrella and tries to open it. Something's stuck. He shakes it once, twice, and finally, in a rage, gives the delicate device a furious yank and … the handle comes off. He angrily tosses away the umbrella, turns determinedly towards the shop entrance, takes a step forward, stops, throws up his arm (the one in which he is not holding the umbrellas), turns on his heel, and continues on his way down the street with five newly repaired, closed, and neatly folded umbrellas under his arm. It just wasn't his day.

At the cathedral I recalled only a face – a stunningly handsome young monk. Handsome, handsome, handsome – hurrying somewhere on a lovely Sunday morning. Undoubtedly to Sunday mass. I don't remember any more what it was I could not forgive him for – for being handsome or for being a monk, or both.

The third stage: Markale market. Across the street from the market, in the building in which the Koštana shoe store was located, from an apartment on the third floor, the flickering of a candle (there's no electricity), the sound of a guitar and of people singing. They have already started to bid farewell to '93. If only we had sent it packing at the moment it first knocked on the doors of Sarajevo. I don't recall the song – I had started to think about the New Year's Eve party that was waiting for me.

The fourth stage: the National Bank on Tito Street. The left entrance. The left half of the granite stairway completely crushed – as though there had never been stairs there. Only bits of stone everywhere on the pavement. Shudders are working their way up my body and fear is climbing up to my throat. I hurry to get away from this place as fast and as far as possible. I wonder who today, on the last day of ill-fated '93, was killed in this place. There are always people passing by here.

The fifth stage: total darkness in the stairwell. The eleventh floor. Behind the doors, silence. People have not yet started to arrive.

In the apartment I was welcomed by a delightful warmth. The hosts were in formal dress. The candlelight would have been romantic if we hadn't known the truth: there had been no electricity for days, and for days more there wouldn't be any. The final flurry of activity before the arrival of the guests. I would have felt as I had in the old days if certain trivial details hadn't been so striking: for example, the fact that the table was set according to all the rules of etiquette, with soup bowls and salad bowls, dinner and dessert plates, glasses for aperitif, wine, water, utensils for hors d'oeuvre, entrée and dessert.

A brief digression: Sarajevans in the past two years have learned to save water, which means this: you have one dish for everything, and after dinner you wipe it clean with bread (if there is any) and you put it away in the sideboard. No more spoons and forks and knives – there's no meat, so you don't have anything to cut, there's no butter, margarine, jam, etc., so you don't have anything to spread – hence for all practical purposes you don't need a knife. Rice can be eaten with a spoon, contrary to all rules of good manners, but good manners are beginning to be a luxury here.

One of my friends, who lives on the thirteenth floor, told me that the six of them eat out of four dishes: her father and mother each have their own dish, and she and her husband and their two children share the remaining two. She and her husband simply can't carry enough water up to the thirteenth floor (no electricity, no elevator, it goes without saying). Her children are small and her parents are old (the father was wounded and lost a leg) and she and her husband both work. She cooks in one pot: she takes care that the food doesn't burn, but actually, there's no danger of that, because she cooks over a fire of newspapers and cardboard which she gathers where she can. There's the occasional piece of wood (a bag of firewood cost them 25 DM, and it was a small bag at that, the kind that in better days used to hold twenty kilograms of potatoes. Just imagine how much wood a twenty-kilo bag can hold). Otherwise, everyone has his or her own teacup, and after use they simply shake it out and turn it over on its saucer until the next day (as there is no sugar, cups can stay "clean" for a long time). Demitasses for coffee are rarely used, and since any such occasion is equivalent to a holiday, they are regularly washed. She has the toughest time with laundry and bedding. She and her husband have been sleeping for months in sleeping bags. Her parents change their linen once a month. The little (four-year-old) girl has only one request: to sleep in sheets with yellow bunnies, of which there is only one set (blue or pink bunnies are out of the question). Her biggest problem is with her son (who is six): ever since a mortar landed in their pantry (in June of '92, the third month of the war which is now in its twenty-first month), he's been wetting his bed. And plastic pants don't help much.

Good heavens, let me at least return to New Year's Eve. I was struck by the magnificent table setting, the decorated room full of candles all burning at the same time. I was also astonished by the spread. There were eleven of us and dinner expenses were evenly shared. I don't know how much that came to – my date was a gentleman. On the menu were foods that I hadn't seen on a table since the beginning of the war, and judging from the comments, neither had the others.

Company started to arrive. A golden oldies tape was playing. One guitar and one violin, one guitarist and one violinist. The atmosphere was pre-war, up until the stroke of midnight.

We congratulated each other on having survived '93, and everyone had only one wish: that we might all survive and stay in one piece in '94 as well. It was terrifying to hear nothing but that ten times: may we stay alive and well and whole, and to hear myself repeat the same thing ten times. I wonder if I will live to see the day when I will wish myself and others a little tiny bit more, and whether I will dare, even if I do outlive this madness, to desire something more.

Somebody put on a classical tape. Beethoven's Fifth Symphony begins, and so does the mortar fire. The horrible ones, the heavy ones, the ones that turn stone into dust. How can I describe to you the sound of the mortar shell that fell right in front of our building or hit the neighbouring one?

The first detonation. The exploding sound of iron demolishing concrete. The walls of the eleven-storey building are shaking, the terrifying sound of glass spilling somewhere outside, the plastic sheeting on the windows is sucked in and then out. The air pressure from the explosion – and in that moment I sense that my palms are soaked in sweat, I feel myself getting cold, and an icy sweat pours over me. My gut tightens, it's no bigger than a fist. I hear my own heart pounding in my chest and throat, and suddenly, the white tablecloth, the dishes, the candles, the people around the table and the whole room recede into the distance at a frightening speed and become tiny and far away. I don't hear people's voices, and the Beethoven is faint and distant. In a moment the scene before me has changed entirely, the room is utterly different, I am somewhere below, my head is resting on my knees, my arms are wrapped around them tightly, squeezing them painfully. Again the tinkling sound of glass, the sound of an entire city of glass being demolished in one instant. Again the terror, grisly, repellent – I don't know where I am, then I sense the knot in my throat loosening, the clenched fingers relaxing, and the terror, like an electrical current, leaving my body. I realize that what I am seeing is just a memory – a flashback to an earlier trauma – of the first big bombing of Sarajevo, when the five of us, my parents, my grandmother, Ilona, and I, sat huddled in a corner of my grandmother's dining room, squeezed in between the table and the wall, listened to the pounding of mortar shells and the shattering of glass, and waited to die.

The scene disappears, the table and the people and the room become bigger, the candlelight brighter and the music louder. The faces around me are serious, they're speaking. I still don't hear voices, everything is still unreal – as though I'm watching a movie. I notice only that some people are getting up from the table and leaving. I feel uncomfortable and dreadfully cold. I feel someone's hand on my arm, a face is approaching me, I hear, finally, I hear a human voice: "Did you have a fright?" I nod, close my eyes, with my fingers I press first my eyeballs, then the bridge of my nose. I open my eyes. My beau, my friend and my love is kissing my hair. I open my eyes. Once again everything is in its place. The sound of conversation reaches me. The mortar explosions blend with the Fifth Symphony to create a music whose score no one will ever write. The music of terror and death and defiance.

The people who left the room took refuge in the hallway in the belief that it would be safer there. To be sure, the apartment is on the eleventh floor, and the windows face the hills where the bombs are coming from.

From the balcony of the apartment the view extends to all four corners of the world: you can see the whole of Sarajevo and all the mountains that surround it. But these mountains, which were once the glory of this city, are now its death. There isn't a Sarajevan who doesn't cast a hateful glance at those hills.

Is it in fact safer in the hallway? Perhaps, but I know a woman who had a shell hit the wall just above her head. She was showered with debris and plaster, nothing more – not even a scratch. She did of course suffer a great shock. Whereas another woman who was situated in the safety of the corridor behind the wall didn't even manage to take fright. She died in the explosion.

Some of us sat around and listened now to the St. Matthew Passion and the mortar rounds. Good old Bach could not have imagined what a phenomenal background to his Passion could be provided by the explosion of tank shells. The flash of the detonations, the sound of glass, air pressure, shock, Bach. A shell has hit the neighbouring high-rise. Ingemar comes into the room and begs us to take cover in the hallway. He is infuriated by our fatalism. Good old Ingemar, our good old Swede. He came to Sarajevo for the first time seven months ago, but he left it too often for the safety of some other universe. We are all fatalists to some extent. The fact that we are alive while so many others, known and unknown, are dead has taught us to believe that survival is a matter of luck or fate, if you will. It's impossible to hide. It's impossible to escape. People here often say that every shell, every bullet has someone's name written on it. Nevertheless, it wasn't fatalism that kept me in my seat. I didn't stay because I believed that one can escape one's fate. I stayed because terror and helplessness engendered defiance. Because defiance awoke pride, and pride became spite. Is there any way that on the first of January, 1994, at 12:25 a.m., I am going to crouch in the corridor while the whole planet is yelling with drunken delight because it is a year older and because indeed it hopes to be younger, lovelier, smarter, healthier, and richer than ever before? Am I about to go down to the basement, so damp and cold and dark, six feet underground, as though I'm already dead? And at the very moment when in five billion of the more fortunate members of my unfortunate race hopes are springing up? And am I about to crawl out of that hole tomorrow into the clear first morning of the new year, crushed and frozen and humiliated, only to be killed by a bomb that reaches me without warning?

You know, Dunja, you don't die from the bomb that you hear, the one that flies over you and whose whistling freezes your blood. You die from the one that is as silent as death itself. There have been cases where a shell has struck a person directly and has blown him apart. He simply disappears. All that's left of him is a bloody porridge scattered over the asphalt and the walls of houses or the carpets of his own bedroom. But that's rare – mostly you die of shrapnel. And you know yourself that one blow from a cleaver is powerful enough to split a beef bone for soup. Now imagine searingly hot, sharp, serrated pieces of steel flying with terrifying speed until they're driven into some soft body. And don't imagine that a piece of shrapnel has to be big to be dangerous. The big ones smash stone as though it were cheese. A little one, a tiny one, half the size of your fingernail, is sufficient not only to kill you, for example, by lodging itself directly in your heart, but also to turn a person into a sieve. An acquaintance of mine had this happen to him. A piece of shrapnel penetrated his thighbone, shot through his pelvis, punctured his intestines (they removed I forget how many metres of fried guts), damaged his liver and his stomach, broke a rib, flew out of his body and landed in the belt of his trousers. The man is alive, he spent months in hospital. When I met him for the first time, he had on a leg brace and walked with crutches. Now he walks without crutches. And off he goes, strolling around town. Out of spite. Spite is a terrible thing. And a dangerous one. Many more people will die on account of it. Yet it is spite and spite alone that keeps alive what little dignity we have left.

Strauss waltzes began, but the explosions did not cease. You hear one far off, and then a second somewhat nearer. That's where the terror starts. You wait for the next one, you know that it will fall even nearer. You start to perspire. The third is dead close. Then you wait for the next one to blow you apart. You wait. You want to run away. You wait. Pressure on your chest. You would like to scream, but you know you won't. You wait. It's unendurable. Instinctively, you hunch up, somehow you want to gather

126

yourself in, make yourself smaller. And again, you wait, you wait, you wait. An explosion. You let out a sigh – it's farther away again. You can't help thinking: whom did it kill instead of me?

My gallant suitor is asking me to dance. Again everything shook, again it's close. Do you think you can't dance a waltz in a room of 1.5 square metres? While fear is crawling up from your stomach, tightening your throat, killing the warmth in your hands, sliding down your back, and while your body is breaking out in an icy sweat? Oh, you can, you can. One shell landed either on the front steps or on the building itself.

I don't know what time it was when the shelling stopped. The guests reassembled and we picked up the party where we left off, if we ever did leave off. The next bout of fairly heavy shelling started about 5:30 a.m. and ended maybe half an hour later.

Around ten in the morning we all went home for a little rest. The agreement was that we would all meet up again at three o'clock for lunch. When I arrived, I found waiting for me the answer to the previous day's question: on the thirty-first of December, at 3:30 p.m., my cousin was killed. She was also my friend and we worked in the same office. She was a brave, cheerful, lovely woman. During the whole war she went to work regularly and walked several kilometres every day. She wasn't afraid, she didn't hide. These last two weeks she did not come to work – she had begun to be afraid. When she finally did show up at the office (two days before her death), she was a totally different person – her face ashen, her eyes sunken and restless, she had lost weight, and there was a peculiar twist to her mouth; she was completely distracted and confused. She kept saying that she was afraid, that she'd lost her nerve, and that she couldn't take it any more. She sensed it coming.

THE TIMES OF LONDON, JANUARY 4, 1994

Shell attack brings carnage
to Sarajevo kindergarten

FROM SRECKO LATAL OF ASSOCIATED PRESS IN SARAJEVO

TWO shells landed in a crowd ▓▓▓▓▓▓▓ who suffered minor leg Emotions boiled in the

127

Dear Dunja,

It is a time of "great expectations" at the Jewish Community Centre, that is, of great anxiety, on account of the preparations for the departure of the convoy. […] You know how much work goes into organizing the departure from Sarajevo of so great a number of people, but now those activities are coming to a *finiš*, at last. I hope that you in Zagreb will soon be welcoming Sarajevans, and that among them will be my sister, because Ilona has decided to "push off" into the world, and I'm happy about that. My one and only wish for her (apart from a successful departure and journey, of course) is that she succeeds in making a life for herself "somewhere out there."

As for me, I still cannot bring myself to leave Sarajevo. I believe I still have the strength to remain in this hell. The Talmud says that the first and basic duty of every human being is to preserve his life. I hope that fate or God will show mercy on me and let me survive. Never before was the idea of the faith of Abraham comprehensible, or more to the point, acceptable to me. Now, in this city and in this time in which death dogs your every step, I realize that faith alone means life. Faith in God, or in life, or in fate, or in oneself – it's all the same. The important thing is to have faith, because it's the only way to escape insanity.

I have to admit, all the same, that I'd dearly love to get out of here, if only for ten days or so, because I detest the feeling that I'm a prisoner here. All of us are, in fact, precisely that – prisoners, sentenced to hard labour, and the feeling that I am not free is worse than the thought that in the very next moment I may not be alive. Leaving and returning would mean something else as well: it would mean defiance. To defy evil, to defy stupidity. It's as though the whole world wants everyone to leave here. All those who decide our lives (I don't know where they get the gall to usurp that right which belongs to God alone, but I must confess, let the Almighty forgive me if He can, that the idea that anyone, even He, might dispose of my life, has never appealed to me), anyhow, all those people seem to want to turn this place into a desert. What will they put on this site instead? What, do you suppose, once there's not a single person left here, or at least not one person in their right mind, what could this place be used for? A junkyard for scrap iron? A huge parking lot? A hat shop? Or the world's largest open-air psychiatric clinic? This last alternative seems to me to be the most appropriate. Besides some few of the present-day locals – the homegrown types, if I may call them that – who will somehow manage to survive, I can list exactly by name all the "wide-world" types whom I would gladly see availing themselves of the services of the aforementioned establishment.

I must be ripe for the loony bin myself when spite is my only motive for staying here, or more precisely, for leaving and returning. I'll have to "get to work" on some such outing to the "outside world," if for no other reason than to see if I can actually *stand* it, if I can *face* the prospect of all the good things it has to offer, for instance, a hot shower in the morning – that would truly be a shock to my system, because thanks to the fact that I live in a part of the city where for the last while, water has been coming every other day, and electricity never, I shower every day with ice-cold water. It's not so terrible. The important thing is not to pull back in the first three seconds. Furthermore, I don't know how I would stand breakfast in some fine hotel with a smorgasbord – you know, where you can choose: juice, then coffee with milk or tea or black coffee, or milk, or tea with milk, then cheese or scrambled eggs, eggs with ham or hard-boiled, soft-boiled, etc., eggs, then this cold cut or that, then jam or honey, or maybe rye or corn or wheat or suchlike flakes, etc., etc. I don't think I could survive Seka's *crêpes fantaisie* or even – imagine! – the very sight of Budapest and one single look at the pastry tray at Gerbeaud's.

Not to mention that I would have a panic attack every time I looked at the masses of people in a market or square in Zagreb. It seems to me that I would constantly be expecting a bomb to fall and to turn the market into a slaughterhouse. You know, ever since the massacre in Vaso Miskin Street, I have not been able to pass normally and calmly through any street where there are a lot of people. Tito Street is always jammed with passers-by, and I always walk down it in a great hurry and don't stop, if I can at all help it, to talk with acquaintances I meet.

And then, before supper, the streetlights would go on. Listen, for me, that would really be an incredible experience. In April it will be two years since I was in a street illuminated with dazzling store displays and street lamps. Now I'm imagining myself at some luxurious *[cosmetics counter in a]* drugstore: creams and lotions, face milk, body milk, face masks and moisturizers, fine soaps, toothpastes, eau de colognes and perfumes, perfumes, perfumes. Toothbrushes. Everything clean, brightly lit, agreeably warm and richly scented. The saleslady all made up.... Ah, no, I've been here long enough.

I am not going to go into a fashion salon nor imagine beautiful hats (I have a weakness for hats), nor fine stockings, elegant shoes, and gloves, too. To say nothing of lingerie.

Enough of this – for a person in my position these are all indecent, not to say perverse, themes.

22 January 1994

Dear Adica!

The past is a billion years away. It is shrouded in fog, as vague as a dream, as a picture we remember liking but which we cannot call to mind.

The present is real, solid and heavy as lead blocks. The present is how to collect some branches, boards, and cartons for firewood, how to haul water, how to scrape together some Deutschmarks for candles. It's this: how to manage to sleep through fourteen-hour nights, how to get ready for a job that demands that you be dressed up and elegant, but you don't have any lipstick, and every day you find on your clothes irrefutable evidence that they played their best roles long ago, it's how to spend six hours in an ice-cold office in wet boots, it's how to escape death and elude terror.

The most endangered are the old people, especially those who have no one to care for them. There are no healthy old people, and for the sick there are no medicines, at least not all kinds and not all the time. With their pension, if they get it at all, they can buy literally nothing – not a box of matches, let alone candles or CANNED FOOD. They depend on that miserable humanitarian aid and on the kindness of their neighbours. Yes indeed, there are Red Cross kitchens, but many of them are in no condition to go there every day, and to beg to someone to go in your stead is a risk few people are prepared to take – the possibility that you might be sending someone to his death is enormous. The bombs don't discriminate and the snipers lie in wait.

The four people killed the day before yesterday were six, not four, and all of them were children. They were sledding. How can you shut a child up in an apartment that is perhaps only marginally safer than the main square? How can you not let him go outside to play in the snow, to go sledding and throw snowballs and have fun? Leila, my classmate from university, has a seven-year-old daughter. She didn't enroll her in school, she won't allow her to play outside with her little friends, she doesn't take her on walks, she doesn't permit her to go out on the balcony – because of the snipers. Minja (that's the child's name) is pale and skinny. Leila was in despair for days after the doctor told her that her little one couldn't get the compulsory vaccination because she is MALNOURISHED – but what in God's name is her mother supposed to nourish her with? Minja is an infinitely melancholy little girl. She is always silent, she flips through old picture books or dresses her Barbie dolls. She never laughs, and her co-ordination is quite poor. My friend is afraid for her child. And tell me, is there anyone on earth who has the right to tell the parents of Sarajevo that their fear is exaggerated? How many mothers and fathers of this city have seen their child dead, dismembered, mutilated? Leila is about to leave Sarajevo along with her daughter. She's leaving behind her husband, parents, friends, job, and apartment, and she doesn't know if she will ever see them again.

Among those children who were killed were two sisters.

The two of us *[Elma and her sister, Ilona]* and our parents are constantly on tenterhooks waiting until a convoy from the Jewish Community Centre pulls out of Sarajevo – on it will be Ilona. It's not exactly a simple thing to see off the sister you have known for some twenty-seven years (it'll be twenty-seven exactly this March). Somehow you've got kind of used to her, you care about her, you worry about her – what can I say? In a word, I love her. Anyhow, you know better than anyone what it's like to see off a sister without knowing when and where you'll ever meet again. For me it's even a little worse than that: I don't know *whether* I'll ever see her again.

As for my own departure – it's not time for me yet. I long to see the closing ceremonies of these bloody Olympic games. If my memory serves, in less than a month's time, in some distant galaxy that is totally inaccessible to me, new Olympic games will begin. I remember those of a decade ago. In those days, from the first moment when my city won the right to host the world right up until the last light was extinguished in Zetra *[Sports Hall]*, I felt myself pulsating like a contented, happy, victorious cell of that organism. I was one of the organizers of the entire figure-skating competition (an official judge), I was a coach for the little figure skaters who brought the games to an end, and I even participated in the closing ceremonies of the Fourteenth Winter Olympic Games – I was one of the four big "Wolfies" *[skaters dressed in costumes representing the wolf mascot of the '84 games]*.

Today, ten years later, I long to escort out of my city this bloody circus. I want to be the one who washes the blood from these streets.

I would ask this one thing of all our fellow Olympic cities: that they consider how possible it is that the show "Sarajevo '92, '93, and '94" could play in their theatres as well. I beg their forgiveness: as God is my witness, I don't wish it upon them, but it is a dreadful fact that there is always someone who does wish it.

Elma

THE NEW YORK TIMES, FEBRUARY 6, 1994

66 Die as Shell Wrecks Sarajevo Market

Toll Is the Worst in 22 Months of Attacks

Dear Caka,

The pictures from Markale *[market]* have gone round the world, and I suppose you've seen them too.

When that mortar shell fell, I was in the street in front of the Jewish Community Centre, standing in front of the bus in which Ilona was sitting, waiting to leave at last this concentration camp of ours. It was 12:30 p.m. when the bomb fell. It registered in my mind as distant and as not particularly powerful. Do you think I wondered where it had fallen or whether it had killed anyone? No. Ilona was in the bus, there in front of me, Mom and Dad were a little farther down the street. And besides, I was too tired, too sad, and too anxious to have the strength to think about just another bomb or just another death in Sarajevo. Only a few minutes later, the police who were guarding the convoy began to disperse the crowd that had gathered to send off their loved ones. That's when I heard that forty people had been killed.

I was neither shaken nor amazed that some Chetnik got the idea to fire a mortar shell into a mass of people. They'd been doing that before as well. Deliberately and precisely. Someone today bought his last kilo of flour, someone else again bought cigarettes for the last time. I felt nothing. Not even gratitude that fate had spared me once again. […] My one and only wish was that Ilona would drive off as soon as possible and that all of us would get off the street.

Among the victims, two familiar names – a neighbour, and the father of a former boyfriend of a good friend of mine. Fifty-six dead – for the moment. Some have not yet been identified because their bodies were horribly disfigured. After all, you could see *[on TV]* headless torsos and a complete set of human entrails on a counter. A market of human meat.

A lot of people I knew left today. Where to – I don't know. Will they return – I don't know. Will I be here waiting for the ones who do return – I don't know. Will I survive – I don't know.

I know only that now I at least have one less worry. Ilona has gone, and once I hear from her tomorrow from Makarska I'll know that at least I won't have to fret about her any more – I do have the idea that the world beyond this bloody barrier is to some small extent safer. But who knows, maybe that too is just another illusion.

16 February 1994

[a continuation of the 5 February letter]
Hi, Caka!
Ilona called from Makarska, though I myself didn't speak with her. But it doesn't really matter. She'd done a little circuit on the Adriatic coast – Makarska – Split – Brela – Split – and after that shot off to Zagreb. She's there now.

People ask me what it's like without her. Does it feel strange, do I miss her? I don't know what to tell them. When the door of the radio station opens, I expect her to walk in. When I come home, I feel sad because I know I won't find her there, and I know just as clearly that she won't come later. In fact, I miss her terribly, but I don't want to dwell on it, because I don't want to burden either myself or those around me. Basically, she's there, I'm here, and surely it's not the end of the world.

Sarajevo is quiet, but also very tense. We're all waiting to see how the world will react *[to the Markale bombing]*. A lot of dust has been raised. For the time being this is good, because the bombs aren't falling. As to where things will go from here, we'll see. I don't set much store by anybody's words, promises, threats, agreements, treaties, or declarations. Nor do I expect anything special. I only hope that the end result of these cannibalistic games will be, for both the global and the local teams, the greatest number possible of healthy survivors. I dare not hope for anything else. But as for believing that the war in Sarajevo is over, that doesn't even cross my mind – I can't afford to play such games with my own nerves. [...] As far as I'm concerned, this war will never end. And if it does end, I'll know how to survive peace too – I hope. Though for me, there will never again exist something which isn't war. Even if I'm sunbathing in Florida or skiing in Switzerland years after the bullets have stopped whistling past my head, I will know that this is only appearance. [...] Peace is a dream that will never be dreamed again.

I said that I wasn't going to write about the atrocity in Markale [market], but I must. The number of dead: 68; the number of wounded: 195.

Dad was telling us that today a patient came to his office with his arm bandaged. What had happened?

– Doctor, I was in the market on Saturday.

– How's that?!

– I went to buy some flour. At the very moment that I was talking with the merchant, there was a flash of light and I felt something slipping down along my arm. I look at my hand, and I see it's nothing. I turn around and I see all this blood. There's blood and body parts everywhere. Then I hear a scream and I feel something dripping down my arm. I look again – blood. That's when I started to run. I wasn't badly hurt. It didn't hit a bone or an artery. But when I got home, Doctor, when I took off my coat, stuck to the back of my coat was human hair, skin, mud, blood. Later I went back to see where the bomb had struck – a metre and a half [ten feet] from where I was standing, doctor. A metre and a half!

THE TIMES OF LONDON, FEBRUARY 19, 1994

Peace plan threatens to freeze division of Bosnian capital

FROM JOEL BRAND IN SARAJEVO

THE same United Nations peace plan that has stopped the hurried talless of over and resolve wanes, the besieging Serbs will still control all the green pen of a British general on peace-keeping duty

25 February 1994

Dear Ilona,

The disaster we trembled in fear of all winter has come to pass: there is no more heating fuel. Of any sort. Of course, our old apple tree is still standing, as twisted and gnarled as ever, awaiting execution. But I still procrastinate. Regrettably, not on sentimental grounds, not because I feel bad about cutting down one fruit tree – there is no place for that kind of sentimentality any longer, not after the experience of the last two years – but

135

rather out of fear of what is to come: we'll have to have something to cook with this spring and summer (assuming we'll have something to cook). As for the following winter, I don't dare even think about it. For the moment we're still getting by with small boards and cardboard boxes, and of course, with the help of a few well-known tricks: I put the rice in water in the morning and leave it to soak all day, so by evening it is so soft that it takes less than ten minutes to cook it over a cardboard fire.

Our bedroom, as you know, is Draught Hotel. […] I'm afraid that this winter I worked myself into a case of frostbite. For at the slightest hint of cold my fingertips start to hurt and my hands go numb and there are times when the pain makes me weep.

The snow has been melting for the last three days. Last night and this morning it rained. Lousy, really lousy weather. Around the eighth, ninth, and tenth of February it snowed as much as it did during the Olympics. That was exactly ten years ago – remember! Only this time no one ploughed the streets, so the snow piled up on the road and sidewalks and turned into ice. There were a lot of injuries, broken arms and legs. Our doctor Asim fell and got a concussion. It's been about two weeks since then, but he still isn't quite right. Well, the snow has been melting for three days and the streets look more like fjords than anything else. The poor townspeople are trying desperately to avoid the biggest puddles, so they plot and calculate their next step, find what looks to be the firmest ground, place their foot on it, and end up in water up to their ankles. One boot can hold twenty gallons of water, I swear! As for the noise on city streets, it's almost intolerable. […] Not because of the cars, or, hmm … streetcars (streetcars – what were those?) but because of the chaotic whooshing, squelching, splashing, gurgling produced by hundreds of thousands of footsteps of people at the edge of despair because with even the tiniest movement water penetrates into their footwear.

If I hadn't been so preoccupied with my own attempts to negotiate my way safely from one more or less secure piece of still icy dry land to another, I would have had a tremendously entertaining time observing my fellow sufferers displaying incredible bravura: stepping high and rather foursquare, and then, right afterwards, making tiny, quick hops, then long leaps, and on and on. All day yesterday I kept seeing scenes from that episode of the Monty Python show, you know, the silly walk contest. Truly wild and wonderful are the ways in which a human being manages to get from point A to point B.

What more can I tell you about our city? From the time of the slaughter in the Markale market and of the, so they say, serious threats from NATO, mortar shells are no longer falling, at least not within "the city limits proper." The streets are overflowing with people, even these last three days of deluge. Risking severe colds and pneumonia (don't forget that the majority have no way of warming up at home, of drinking hot tea and drying their shoes, because there is gas in some places and not in others, there's no heating anywhere, and only the lucky few have electricity), people nevertheless stroll along and examine the wares on the stands, on tables and stools and suchlike ranged along Vase Strasse *[Vaso Miskin Street; the German form of "street" seems to be used for the sake of the rhyme]*, which is to say, the sorrowful street of spite.* And here you can find anything – from a needle to a locomotive, anything, that is, except what you actually need. Porcelain coffee services, crystal bowls, dessert forks with the coat of arms of Vienna, hair dyes, new and used shoes, coats, pants, valves for natural gas and other items necessary for gas installations, Ninja turtles, Barbie dolls, rat poison and mousetraps, electric coffee mills and mixers (who could possibly need those – when there's no coffee, no electricity, and certainly no sugar), threads and wools, thick woollen socks, acrylic slippers, hair bows, plush toys, etc., etc. Everything, of course, costs Deutschmarks, so I don't linger too long. Even for necessities I don't have – you know what – Deutschmarks.

There are lots of tables of books: from biographies of Tito to Russian classics and Joyce to the newest American bestsellers (you have to take "newest" with a grain of salt, because time stopped for us two years ago – since that time we've had no idea what is being read, written, painted,

---

*After the breadline massacre of May 27, 1992, Vaso Miskin Street became popularly known as Ulica Prkosa, "Defiance Street."

composed, invented, discovered, built, filmed in the world) to women's magazines and various cookbooks along the lines of *The Great National Cookbook*: "Into a bowl add twelve egg yolks ..." – oh, sure, that's about fifty marks right there, at least going by the prices of a month ago, and as far as I remember, it's been at least that long since I've even seen an egg at the market. (Wait, let's see how long it's been since I've eaten one. I know exactly: from last Passover, and that's a year ago.)

I get a real kick out of looking at those cookbooks ("Add a few Indian walnuts ..."), because I can't even make a decent soup any more, that is, every soup tastes like a pizza that's been through a dozen rinses – all that's left of our household spices is marvellous oregano. When it comes to spices, our cupboards are definitely bare.

The spirit that reigns among us "patriots" is a kind of mixture of euphoric happiness and exalted pessimism (you figure out what that could possibly mean). The majority of the people with whom I speak think that the war in Sarajevo is over. They're all somehow preparing for peace, that is, they all insist that mortar shells will no longer kill in the streets of Sarajevo and in schoolyards, in the squares and by the wells, in bread lines, in apartments and houses. You know your sister too well to believe that she would give herself over to such ill-considered optimism. It doesn't wash with me. The only statement I could commit myself to would be Tertullian's *credo quia absurdum* (I believe because it is impossible – what is possible does not require faith); only in that way could I believe that Death has finished her banquet at this "groaning board." If it isn't mortar shells, it will be something else. If we turn towards Europe, we'll have the Italy of years ago or else Ireland (oh, what a short memory Europe has, in what an imbecile fashion it puffs up its chest at its democracy), or if we cast only a fleeting glance towards the Orient, in the violet morning mist we will behold Lebanon.

Mom has been terribly anxious during this peaceful period in Sarajevo. She says she can't stand the silence, because she's always waiting for something to happen. Dreadful! Truly, we'll all be walking around demented from now until kingdom come.

Here's the most recent Sarajevo joke:

Karadžić arrives at the Pearly Gates. St. Peter says to him:

– You, go on down!

– But why? Please, Pete, I beg you, I'm not that bad.

– Look, I said down! It's hell for you!

– But …

– DOWN!

After some time St. Peter sends an angel down to see what Karadžić is up to. The angel comes to the gates of hell and sees a pair of gloomy devils huddled in front of the gates.

– What are you doing here? Why aren't you inside?

– We're refugees.

Here's another joke, old as the Greeks, but its message is apt:

A Scotsman prayed to God for years to let him win the lottery jackpot. He prayed and he prayed, one year, two, five, and finally, after ten years the heavens opened and God shouted in exasperation:

– So, buy a ticket, already!

You got the point, didn't you? Okay. Now just keep it in mind.

THE TIMES OF LONDON, MARCH 1, 1994

Four Serb jets shot down by Nato

9-minute action
s alliance's first
taste of battle

2 M a r c h 1 9 9 4

Dear Dunja!

In Sarajevo spring has begun. Perhaps even peace as well! Since that atrocity in Markale market bombs have not been falling on the city itself. People have become more relaxed, and even those for whom optimism is not their long suit are beginning to hope that Sarajevo will cease to be a slaughterhouse. The streets are full of people. Garbage is being picked up from the sidewalks. The containers *[dumpsters, storage bins, etc., set up to screen pedestrians from sniper fire]* that have been shot up by snipers are being removed from intersections. It seems to me that all this has come too quickly and that this is just one more pause. I'm not telling you this on the basis of some scholarly analyses or of accurate knowledge of the political or military situation in this out-of-the-way back yard of ours, or else of a familiarity with the world situation. It is my fear speaking. I don't dare believe in the good, because I'm afraid that a repeated outbreak of evil would annihilate me definitively. I have always said about myself that there is no misfortune that I won't be able to endure, if for no other reason than out of sheer bloodymindedness – I'm a fighter, very often a Don Quixote; in any case, my *spiritus movens [motivating spirit]* has always been struggle – pro and con this or that. Yet I often ask myself: where are my limits? Is there a limit to human strength, and if there is, where is mine? You know, as I think about this, my insides begin to tremble, rebellion rises from my stomach and seeps into every one of my cells.

As I was saying, in Sarajevo people are breathing more easily. They are coming to life. They're starting to make plans for the future. The colourful stalls of street vendors remind me of India – a sea of gewgaws and gadgets that the vendors are promoting, trying to convince potential customers that a meat grinder is the very thing they absolutely need (can you believe that neither my mother nor I have bought meat for almost two full years now) or that this is precisely the right moment to buy a synthesizer. As a matter of fact, those who do have money could now get high-quality stuff for a very low price. A sound system that used to cost 5,000 DM before the war is now going for 500. You can get a PC 286 computer for 1,000. Not to mention valuable antique jewellery – it's selling for next to nothing. In some cases the goods are stolen; in others the owners are compelled to sell because they have no other means of buying food. People who have decided to leave here for good are selling beautifully furnished apartments for about 10,000 DM. I was inside one such apartment, four bedrooms, two floors, without major damage, with complete furnishings, some from Italy or Austria, some assorted Djordjević pieces *[from a firm specializing in ornate antique-style furniture]* – it's going for 12,000 DM, and that in two installments, 6,000 down and the rest when the buyer can come up with it. I forgot to say that the price includes a garage.

Things like this are already familiar to us, we've read about them. Poverty, grinding poverty. If I ever have enough money for luxuries I will never spend it on anything that I can't put in my pocket. As far as the pleasures of the mind are concerned – I'll borrow books from libraries, I'll listen to music at concerts, and my children will play the mouth organ, assuming I get up the courage to have any.

But who knows? The human being is a peculiar little beast – it forgets quickly and easily, and of all living creatures it is the most easily adaptable. So even though I don't want to forget even one single moment of the past two years, it is highly likely that I will behave exactly the same as those people whose only wish is to erase from their memory all this suffering, terror, and misery as quickly and as effectively as possible. The observation that history repeats itself is merely proof of the incredible human need to forget.

You know, I think back on Romania, the fall of the Berlin wall, the Gulf War, the breakup of the USSR – the world was changing and I knew that war would not pass us by either. I kept insisting to my parents, half in jest, half in earnest: Sell your home, go to New Zealand! Yet nevertheless, on Friday, April 3, 1992, moments before the beginning of the conflict in Sarajevo, I was certain that nothing would happen and that the news of the war, which in fact had already started in Sarajevo, was only rumour.

And now many people assure me that there will be no more deaths from shelling here. That Sarajevo has seen the end of the war. Well, we'll see.

All this irresistibly reminds me of the joke about the flea:

A young biologist is doing an experiment to see how far a flea can jump. He puts it on the table, taps beside it with his finger, and shouts:

– Jump, flea!

The flea jumps six centimetres. He writes down: A flea with six legs jumps six centimetres. The biologist pulls off one of its legs, puts it on the table, taps again, and shouts:

– Jump, flea!

The flea jumps five centimetres. This time he writes down: A flea with five legs jumps five centimetres. The great scientist keeps pulling off its legs and measuring until he gets to the last one. He pulls it off, puts the flea on the table, taps, and yells:

– Jump, flea!

The flea doesn't move.

– Jump, flea!

Nothing.

The genius writes down: A flea with no legs can't hear!

The single difference between our experiment and the one with the flea is that in that case, only one flea suffered, whereas here, there are hundreds of thousands of people. In the name of what? – I'll be damned if I know!

In Sarajevo it has been peaceful for almost a month, and spring is coming.

1 3   M a r c h   1 9 9 4

Dear Ilona,

I must confess that my concentration is nil – outside it's a gorgeous day, it's very warm, you can hear birds singing and people walking and talking in the streets.

It looks as though this spring weather is no joke, and this peace has already made a serious show of lasting. The people that I meet, both acquaintances and strangers, are full of energy and hope. The streets are clean, new stores and cafés are opening, tables are being set up in miniature gardens on the sidewalks and in the parks. Just think, one day recently I bought cigarettes at a kiosk here in Bjelave – like in the good old days, except that I paid for them with Deutschmarks.

Some new long-legged beauties are walking about town. Some new handsome youths are courting them. On the streets there are more and more automobiles and here and there traffic lights are being repaired. The street vendors' stalls are filled to overflowing with everything imaginable

(I've already written about that), but what is new is that the municipal authorities in some parts of the city are already starting to remove them from the streets. Isn't that ludicrous – while the bombs were falling, it's as though no one minded that masses of potential corpses were flocking around these tables while the former premises of retail outlets echoed emptily, but now ... it's as though the city has actually started to function like a city. No doubt this is only a temporary development, but I will say it's an enjoyable one.

The Market is packed – with merchandise, merchants, and customers. In any case it was always crowded in the Market, but now, besides food from aid shipments, candles, and cigarettes, you can also buy oranges, kiwis, chickens – when the day before yesterday I saw a cantaloupe, I couldn't believe my own eyes, and I'm still wondering whether I was mistaken, and it wasn't some unusual kind of squash, because I don't remember ever seeing – not just in the last two years, but ever in my life – a cantaloupe in Sarajevo in March. But perhaps I've already forgotten it all. To tell you the truth, I'm having serious problems with my memory – the time before the war keeps getting foggier and seems dreadfully far away – I have an easier time remembering historical dates that I learned from textbooks than the significant dates in my own life. Not to harp on the point, that whole past, all the thirty years of my life before April '92, was such a banal charade, or (why prettify it?) it was such a vile deception, that it doesn't even matter any more what happened.

I have been deceived because I thought I had a country, and that it was the best and most stable country in the world, but that same country is falling apart like a house of cards. I have been deceived because I believed that there exists brotherhood among people, but these people have been killing each other. In fact, upon second thought, there actually do exist *bona fide* brotherly relations – after all, Cain killed Abel (provided that the current mania for overhauling everything hasn't prompted someone to come up with a New Old Testament). I have been deceived because I thought that first of all there appeared Humans, and only afterwards Serbs, Croats, Muslims, Chinese, etc., but it turns out that the latter came first, whereas the former doesn't even exist – the Human Being has not yet been born.

143

God has not yet created him. We are simply some sort of (God help us!) creatures. Better luck next time, or, as we say here – third time lucky.

Etc., etc., etc. So, to make a long story short, it turns out that the war is the most valuable of all the gifts that have been lavished upon me thus far by God, my parents, and politics – I mean that the war has stripped away the façades: my homeland doesn't exist, tolerance doesn't exist, see, there aren't even human beings, at least not the kind there ought to be according to God's childish plan. Forgive me, Lord, but you were putting us on. But you won't forgive me, for if you knew how to forgive, so would your offspring.

Ilona, I don't know what to tell you about this peace – it's arrived as though for real. I just don't know how long it intends to stay.

THE TIMES OF LONDON, MARCH 9, 1994

Sarajevo hails rattle of returning trams

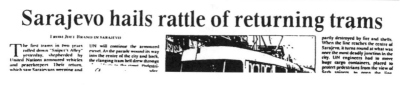

14 March 1994

[a continuation of the 13 March letter to Ilona]
Tomorrow the streetcars will be operating and there will be ten vehicles in service. I'm going to try to go for a ride tomorrow – it'll be the first time in almost two years, more precisely, in twenty-three months.

15 March 1994

The streetcars really did start up today; I didn't ride on one, but I saw it – I went home from the Jewish Community Centre via Obala Street, and before I could turn onto Radičević Street – I caught sight of a streetcar turning around at Skenderija! It looked both unreal and so familiar! The red streetcar appeared between the houses in Valter Perić Street. It went straight, then, at the bend, it lurched a bit and started to turn around. I don't know how to describe to you exactly what I felt. I know only that for an instant I felt terror, the kind we feel in the semi-darkness of a house in which we are alone, and suddenly, someone's silhouette flits past us. Only a fraction of a second later we realize that we were frightened by our own image in a mirror we had passed, and we breathe a sigh of relief and sense a pleasurable tingling as the dread takes leave of our body. Well, that's the kind of fear that overwhelmed me, because I wondered: Lord, surely I won't discover that none of all those terrors that I survived were actually real?

I mentioned to you that I went via Obala Street. Imagine, along Obala Street, people aren't going, they're strolling. Slowly, one foot before the other, they look around at the damaged houses, the snapped streetcar wires, the holes in the retaining wall of the Miljacka and the large pieces of stone in the water. All the same, they often cast a glance at Mt. Trebević, green, but with a horribly thinned-out forest, clearly visible in the bright spring sunshine and still frightening. Then they quicken their pace and turn their head to the other side, for they know: from above someone is nevertheless watching them, and is doing so, without a doubt, through the sights of a sniper's rifle.

I went along slowly and looked at that mountain for a long time, not taking my eyes off it, and I remembered how last winter, I used to go that way to work, hoping I was concealed by the fog, my senses sharpened so that I could hear and perceive the first shot directed at me or else fired just like that, at random; hoping that that first one at least would miss me and that I would have enough time to escape the next one, praying to God that I would reach my office as soon as possible, uninjured, and with a sense of dreadful discomfort at the thought that I would have to turn off onto one of the streets protected from the snipers' view, but still dangerous because of the mortar shells which were falling daily on all the streets at all hours of the day and night. The memory still fills me with unease and a need to stop, the sooner the better, even thinking about that time. But see, today I went along there slowly, exposed to anyone's view, and I recalled last December and the December of '92 and I forced myself to think about that terror, to feel it anew, so that I would never forget it.

Forgetfulness is dangerous, as are memories, for that matter.

[a continuation of the 13 March letter to Ilona]

So, on Friday I decide that I'm finally going to go for a streetcar ride from Skenderija to the depot. I leave the office with Aida and the two of us set out, slowly, step by step, she homewards, and I to the stop on Maxim Gorky Street. Do you know which way we went? We took the shortest route down Miss Irby Street and through the park behind the Presidency. We look at Skenderija and at Mount Trebević behind it. And we don't hurry, we don't speed up our pace. (Do you remember when that sniper fired at us by the bridge and we stood for five minutes behind the columns of the building on the other side of the road from the bridge, not daring to run even to the main door? What fun it was standing there, each of us behind her column, not knowing which was the smarter thing to do: to make a run for it across the bridge or to run back towards the Presidency.) Anyhow, why go on about it – the vista extended towards Mt. Trebević, the park spread itself out before us, and the two of us walked along laughing. Right then the streetcar appeared, and (picture this) figuring that I'll have a long wait till the next one, I say a quick goodbye to Aida and run to catch this one – like in the old days. Man alive! It was just fantastic! A good old Sarajevo custom: racing for the streetcar, and not running for your life across lethal intersections. I couldn't believe myself and I was laughing at myself. To be honest, I must confess that I had pictured this first re-entry into my favourite means of public transit as a much more solemn affair, something like this: I slowly approach the streetcar stop, my senses sharpened, the very incarnation of vigilance, primed for every detail, for every scene from this august occasion, for every emotion evoked in me by this venerable custom. I had wished to capture the movements of the people waiting at the stop, the way they approached the streetcar, their faces, their reactions, their comments. I had wanted to get a good look at the driver and the tracks and the wires and the advertisements covering the flanks of this marvel of technology! And instead of all this – I'm racing to catch it and seeing nothing except that the streetcar is almost here and that I'll probably make it. Well, who wouldn't laugh?!

I leapt in and even managed to find a seat, and what's more, on the very side that I had decided would be the more interesting: the left side, facing Grbavica. By now I had somewhat pulled myself together and started to look around. There were lots of kids – for the last two days, riding the streetcar has been their favourite pastime. Boys between eight and twelve or thirteen years of age go from one vehicle to another. They get on at the first stop, and then the comments and discussions begin: what's the number of the streetcar (I don't mean the number of the route, but rather the number of the vehicle – it seems they have already figured out how to tell one vehicle from another); who's a good driver and who isn't; how long does it take to go from one stop to the next, and the like; at which stop are they going to get off, and once they do get off, are they going to continue along the same route on the next streetcar or are they simply going to cross the street and come back? And the whole group of them won't get off at the same stop, just two or three at a time, and then they meet up again, and so it goes for the rest of the day.

The adults are more preoccupied with themselves: some behave as though there was never a time when they didn't return from work on the streetcar, while others look all around in astonishment. Naturally, a variety of remarks are made, some witty, some bitter. Some people frown and fidget, cursing and threatening the children who are forever milling about and pushing their way through the crowd.

When Municipal Transport Vehicle No. 1 finally got going, there was a new shock: the traffic lights by the Department of Health were working. Actually working: red, yellow, green! For the second time in the last five or six days I was gripped by the fear that I was losing my mind and for the second time I wondered whether what I thought happened actually did happen: had there indeed been a war or had I made the whole thing up? Something was not quite right. Either with me or with those traffic lights – in God's name, how could this be, a traffic light that works? It is logical that if you want to regulate traffic at an intersection, traffic lights are necessary, yet it is difficult to believe that we truly have come this far.

My fear that I had imagined this war vanished as soon as we reached the old Military Hospital. The bare outer walls with holes for windows and

147

doors, with no dividing walls or roof, reassured me that I was not crazy after all. Whatever wood there had been on these walls had already disappeared during the first winter; people quite simply carried off even the last splinter to save themselves from freezing to death and to be able to cook something to eat.

Next came the appalling sight of Marijin Dvor. The old tobacco factory had completely burned down, its roof gone and the ceilings between the storeys collapsed – just one more ruin. [...] And then the Holiday Inn – holes in the concrete wall. Luckily, it's still recognizably yellow.

The Executive Council building – eerie, black, burned out. Around it a pile of glass and debris. Between it and the Faculty of Philosophy was stretched some reddish UNPROFOR sheeting, torn and riddled with holes. It was supposed to prevent a sniper from taking aim through his scope, but it was no protection against a bullet fired at random. The Technical School was heavily damaged, and the street between the Technical School and the barracks looked like something out of one of those cataclysmic science-fiction films – a dead city from a perished civilization. A chaos of broken streetcar wires, glass, and assorted debris on the deserted sidewalks and roadway.

And on the left side, behind the university and the museum, across the river Miljacka: Grbavica. So near, and yet infinitely far. So familiar, and so appalling. A different country. And a hostile one. And right in the middle, between these two enemy states, the bridge, which today still divides them, will be open. And then the inhabitants of Grbavica will be able to visit their relatives in this part of the city, and those of us over here will be able to visit them. A tragedy and a farce at the same time. Don't think for a moment that there will be free passage for anyone who wants to come here or go there. You'll need a pile of papers, all kinds of certificates and permits. Nobody can visualize exactly what it will be like. Today I heard that they're going to let through fifty people at a time in either direction. Those going from here to there will be taken to the Boško Buha Pioneers' Centre. On fifty chairs at one end of the hall will sit the visitors, and on another fifty chairs at the other end, those who are being visited. How visits to our side will be organized, I can't say; I'm not even sure whether the preceding information about Boško Buha is accurate.

How awful, awful, awful! Can you imagine what these meetings will be like? Aida will go to visit her mother. Someone will come to see his brother. And how many people will there be who come full of anticipation and joy, hope and fear, and who find out on that day that their loved ones are no longer among the living? How many parents and children will not be able to recognize each other? And how many of them will never again be able to understand each other and may never again be able to accept each other?

Madness! I wonder how much time will pass before people will be able to travel freely back and forth? If this galloping peace is not merely an illusion, it may be very soon. That possibility leaves me speechless. Not, however, with joy, but rather with terror and bafflement. Did it really need to cost 300,000 lives (this figure has not been confirmed) to ensure my free passage across the Brotherhood and Unity Bridge so I can go to the Grbavica market and buy potatoes? Let them forgive me who can for what I am about to say, but the phrase "brotherhood and unity" today sounds revoltingly hypocritical to me. A bold-faced lie, cotton candy, a cheap gimmick. [...] Not to mention the vile taste of taking this divided city, in which there has been so much savage destruction and killing, and once again, for the first time in two years, linking it with the people who have been doing the destroying and killing; and all thanks to this brave new slogan that once held so much promise. One more splendid vision turned to ashes through human stupidity.

Should I continue to describe for you the ruins – the walls of the School of Economics or of the building across the street from it, partially black from the blazes that roared through tens of apartments, and horribly damaged, etc., etc.? I cannot weary you with more because I cannot find new words for the same horror and woe.

At the last stop I got off the streetcar and crossed over to the left bank of the Miljacka – that's a part of the city I haven't been through in the past two years, except for the one time I was in Pero Kosorić Square. That was in the fall of '92 and walking around there was fairly hazardous – every day someone would be hit by a sniper, and there were days when several people at a time would be killed in the same place: they were the victims of a lunatic who was practising marksmanship with moving targets – people.

149

The story was that that quarter was the territory of a Romanian woman, a hired gun, who for months sowed terror and death. They say that she killed mainly men, and older ones at that.

Pero Kosorić Square at that time looked ghostly. Charred high-rises and destroyed buildings, punctured by shells like old, rust-eaten tin cans; on a cold, murky, rainy late autumn day, they resembled a region devastated by an ancient cataclysm in a long extinct galaxy. There were no people, no automobiles, no sign of life, yet there were still people there, huddled behind the precarious walls of their demolished apartments, and life flowed on there nevertheless.

A few days ago that place looked different. The high-rises were still black, the buildings no less damaged, but the day was lovely and warm, and there were people walking in the streets, children were riding bicycles or were on roller skates, and there were mini-markets on the walks. Merchants or black marketeers or the unfortunate, honest people and crooks were selling oil and canned food, eggs and margarine, coffee and chocolate and who knows what else. Mind you, that "market" was not in the square itself, but rather somewhat farther down on one of the smaller bridges over the Miljacka, and it reminded me of India and the brightly coloured stalls with merchandise heaped up on cloths spread on the pavement. But that was India, and from what I was able to see of Europe, central, western and eastern, Sarajevo was miles, thousands of miles removed from the poorer quarters of Delhi, and closer to a Vienna or a Venice. But in the course of the last two years in the new quarters of Sarajevo, paupers' stalls have sprung up. I am sure that a journalist on assignment in Sarajevo, one who has never been in the city before, coming from some cosy, relatively stable country, could not have the slightest inkling of what has happened here.

The green spaces around the city and the little parks are no longer green. Now they are carefully tended plots, dug-up and seeded patches from which will spring onions, lettuce, beets, tomatoes.... Women and men and children of all ages are digging, crumbling the soil, collecting stones and rubbish, pulling weeds. Some are obviously not handy with garden tools, others are highly skillful. The plots are marked off with little metal stakes, with wire brought from who knows which ruin, some metal and plastic strips whose original purpose I could in no way determine, and ordinary strips of old sheets and rope. One family had cordoned off their little garden with a low wall of neatly piled stones – I don't know where in these concrete housing complexes they found so many ordinary stones. What will grow and how in these oases between ten-storey buildings, I don't know.

Let me just mention further that no one has marked off their little garden with boards, branches, or shrubbery – either the second winter of war swept them all away, or else they're being saved up, God forbid, for the next.

Thus I roamed between the buildings and along the Miljacka. The people I encountered were fairly relaxed. Oh, no, I won't speak of any sort of optimism or happiness or other saccharine claptrap – we've got a long way to go yet, if we ever reach that frame of mind at all – but people were quite simply more relaxed, more easygoing than, say, two months ago. I won't say that they were less tired – the faces of the people I see are infinitely weary, whether they are smiling or sombre. We are all tired, to the point of exhaustion. And our weariness will go on increasing, even if this very moment should usher in everywhere a lasting and stable peace.

Here's one more vignette of Sarajevo life. A tiny children's playground, set up among tall buildings. A cement slab, and around it a lawn (which has not yet been dug and parcelled up). In the playground a toboggan, two seesaws and two swings. At one end an enormous heap of garbage – tin cans, plastic bags, an old electric range, broken glass bottles, a piece of a tattered old Bosnian kilim rug (its owner must have had no problem with heating, and it could not have been left here very long ago, because no one has picked it up for fuel), a rusted old car door – in a word, a huge pile of old junk and debris. At the opposite end two completely bombed-out automobile wrecks, one atop the other on the lawn, right at the edge of the playground. On the ground an ocean of broken glass, here and there a bullet casing. The toboggan a hollow frame – the wooden boards doubtless warmed someone up a little, the seats on the swings are missing, on the two seesaws there is only one seat. And three children and one daddy. A sweet little blond boy is pulling along on a thin string some sort of little plastic truck with its wheels missing, and he's babbling to himself. The other two children are playing on the seesaw – the slightly bigger one is sitting directly on the metal pipe, and his daddy is holding on to him, while his mind is far away. The man is tall, thin, neatly shaven, a little hunched over; his gaze has settled somewhere in front of him, and who knows what thoughts he's turning over in his head. The third child, with a shock of blond hair on the top of her head, is sitting at the other end of the seesaw and clutching the handle firmly in her little hands. She is the merriest member of the family. She is laughing, and every time she swings up or down, she opens wide her unbelievably black eyes. Blond hair, a pale complexion, and black, black eyes. An incredible scene. In the midst of all that chaos and filth, children are playing. Daddy has taken them to the park. Everything is normal and everything is so wrong.

I mentioned children. There are an enormous number of them outside, lured out by the sun and the peace. But all those children are pale, mostly skinny, and with noticeable dark circles under their eyes. What's on their minds, what sort of games they're playing, what their world is like after these past two years – I don't know. A colleague of mine, an educational consultant, told me about the response of a ten-year-old to what was happening around him. It was in the context of some psychological test. Children were given a sheet of paper divided into four sections. The first section was labelled "The Past": here they were supposed to draw a picture related to their past experience. Next was the present, then the future, and lastly, a square in which they were supposed to comment on their current situation. Their pictures of the past were, on the whole, full of bright colours and cheerful themes. The present was drawn in grey and black, with lots of bombs and images of death. The boy I'm talking about did pretty much the same thing as the others, with this difference: he left the square marked "The Future" completely blank – he didn't draw a single line. And where he was supposed to write something, he put down: "*Nemaš brineš i tako ćeš da pogineš*" – "Don't worry, don't bother, they'll kill you one way or the other."

Let's go on. I wandered between the buildings and returned to the path

152

along the Miljacka. I encountered fewer and fewer people and more and more garbage. Once again a park turned over to spring gardening chores. I came to a small market near the bridge by the Electric Company building. Here I was stopped by a sentry: "Do you live in that building?" he asked me, indicating a nearby building behind him.

"No, I don't."

"Show me your papers."

I took out my ID and gave it to him. He asked me what I was doing. I replied that I was simply going for a walk.

"This is a war zone. You can't go any further."

"Come on, isn't the whole city a war zone? Fine. I was hoping to be able to cross the bridge. In fact I wanted to see where I would get stopped, how far you can go on this side."

"Well, you've come to the end. But this is not a wise thing to do. People have got careless. But just you wait – one moment and…. Draw back a little behind the wall. There, where you're standing, not seven days ago a sniper killed a youth. They're always watching. They're watching you now."

"I presumed as much." I cast a glance towards Mt. Trebević, and the uneasiness I always feel out in the open increased. But I didn't draw back. Don't ask me why not. You know me, out of spite. Stupid, childish, irrational spite. Often I'm afraid of my own desire and need, yes, a real need to tempt fate. I am exploring the limits of my own luck and of God's patience and mercy. What is this self-destructive urge in my being, and in human beings in general, for it seems to me that all too many people are inclined to such stupid, unnecessary experiments? Experiments without any purpose. […] I am almost certain that everyone, every citizen of this bizarre city, some consciously, others unconsciously, feel the need to play Russian roulette. How else can one explain the streets filled to overflowing at the very time when bombs were falling, day in and day out, in every corner of this city? How can one explain why people went, literally under bombs and between them, to public gatherings – to the theatre, to concerts? How, furthermore, can one explain why I myself know more than a few people who, several times a day, without any real need, ran across the

153

most dangerous intersections, even though they could have gone by some other, admittedly longer, but on that account safer, route (safety – an appallingly relative notion)? When, in fact, there was no hurry. [...] Not to mention the fact that every day at fifteen minutes to two, I would leave the office to go for lunch at the Jewish Community Centre, and not because I was hungry, because I could have eaten at work as well, but so that I wouldn't break with a certain "tradition." And it didn't matter that a shell landed at sixteen minutes to two at the very entrance of my place of work and that we knew from experience that shells would fall in at least two more places in the vicinity. And it didn't matter that near Svjetlost [*publishing company*] shrapnel was hissing past and landing in the puddles around me, or that for the second time I came across a corpse by the same Svjetlost building while the smoke from the mortar shell was just clearing. Oh, I'm guilty of a host of such stupidities, and now, when the shells are no longer falling and the snipers have settled down, I'm being defiant all over again. Defying whom and why? I don't know.

I chatted a little longer with the sentry. I asked him if I could take [*President Woodrow*] Wilson Street. "Why, for God's sake? I went that way once last year in August, but I was drunk. I wouldn't do it sober for anything in the world. But there are people like that – they slip through somehow and come to that bridge and stand in the middle of it, they talk to themselves and stare out somewhere. We yell at them to get off, but they pay no attention, they just stand there, and then they go away. A few months ago, some guy came and stood on the bridge. From above, a sniper was firing – all around him. If he'd wanted to kill him, he would have knocked him off with the first shot. He was just having a little fun, but this guy stood there, cool as ice, and stared into the water. There'll be more of us like that – wacko – all the time."

I said goodbye to the fellow, headed back, and at the very next bridge – I didn't take Wilson Street.

I won't tell you about the remainder of my journey – it's pointless to start on again about the ruins. I'll just tell you that I stopped for a second at the Brotherhood and Unity Bridge and cast a glance across the border. On the bridge was UNPROFOR.

154

What more can I tell you? I went to Zetra and to the stadium. Mind you, I'd been by there several times during the war, only I went slowly this time, trying to memorize every detail. Zetra, like a crumpled and charred sheet of copper. It looks hideous. Around it lawns converted into gardens. I couldn't go inside – UNPROFOR was there. The stadium is still green, children were playing soccer.

The graveyards are horrifying. There are few old graves even though they stopped burying people there quite a while ago. Every square foot of land has been utilized. The auxiliary stadium is almost filled up with graves. I went to my *[maternal]* grandmother's grave. Immediately next to it was buried Vedrana Glavaš* (1989–1992) – the little girl who was killed in the bus which was supposed to take the children from the orphanage to Germany.

I wrote down a few more names and dates: Roki Sulejmanović** (1991–1992); Gološ Adem** (1973–1992); Duraković Bajro** (1958–1992); Siniša Vidaković** (1970–1992), etc.

2 2   M a r c h   1 9 9 4

[a continuation of the 13 March letter]

I wonder why I feel obliged to write "Sarajevo" – as though I could be writing you from some other place.

Here is the text below a photograph in *Oslobođenje* in which you see two men repairing street lamps in Vaso Miskin Street: "Soon the streets of the city will once again be illuminated by the glow of streetlights." There's nothing for me to do but believe it – what can I do? The traffic lights have started working, I'm regularly running for the streetcar (twice today), there's electricity, there's water, there's gas.

There's a soccer tournament going on here, every so often a new theatre première appears, there are more and more advertisements on radio and television.

*Serbian name.
**Muslim names.

155

Automobiles are once again driving only in one direction, and in the right one to boot, and they've announced the reconstruction of the streetcar network from Skenderija to Baščaršija, which is to say that the greater part of the city will be covered by streetcar service. The reconstruction is supposed to take two weeks.

23 March 1994

Today the bridge really was opened. I wasn't there, and there's no point in my describing the TV report to you; you've probably already seen the same thing.

The first bus has set out on the Sarajevo–Butmir–Hrasnica–Sarajevo line.

The first bus has set out on the Sarajevo–Zenica–Sarajevo line.

Who knows, maybe you and I will see each other soon.

5 April 1994

My darling sister,

It was two years ago that we ran down to the basement for the first time with our backpacks and blankets. That was the first time that a bomb fell on Bistrik and we became aware for the first time of the war that already existed around us, but it hadn't yet hit home.

You left Sarajevo on the last day of the war here. At least for now it looks that way. There's no longer any shooting, shells aren't falling, people are riding the streetcars, washing machines are humming away, very few people still have to draw water every day from wells, there is natural gas (on the whole), about ten this morning in Tito Street the street lamps lit up, and the same thing happened the evening before last.

The city is beginning to function like a city.

People are reacting to this peace in a variety of ways. From enthusiasm to despair. The sort of thing we used to talk about while we were slipping our way under and between the bombs – how we would fully feel the consequences of the horror we were then undergoing only when the war

156

stopped and we started to relax – has now become a reality. Many acquaintances that I meet complain they have lost their motivation, they no longer desire to take part in anything, they're tired. They spend hours in front of the television or else they sleep. Some are starting to lose weight again.

The enthusiasts, on the other hand, are talking of the golden age that is at hand; they're full of faith and confidence. They go out of their way to join every gathering, of which there have been many these last few days, and to have a hand in every project that's even rumoured to be underway or to be worth starting.

The entrepreneurial types are starting to carry out their plans for making money.

But everyone, these three groups and all the rest, are somehow stuck. Everybody is in a state of expectancy. Everyone is aware that the war in Bosnia is not over, but also that now something new is beginning. And again, something unknown.

How long will it last, this waiting, this straining, this hoping or despairing? Some will probably spend the next thirty or fifty years of their lives waiting to make a definitive end of something or a definitive beginning.

There will be a lot of lost people, a lot of lost souls in this city. And in this country and in all the unfortunate countries which were once one, and which will one day be who knows what. But doubtless someone does know, someone who will put forward a plan for phase B, C, D ... etc., of the project entitled "Ex-Yugoslavia." Someone probably does know, but it isn't you or I.

Many people with empty shells of lives are walking along these crowded streets, but there are also many who have become stronger and whom the experience of the past two years will enable to attain much more than they would have had there not been a war.

"And yet it moves," said Galileo. It's all a question of catching the right streetcar. Which one is the right one, however, is anyone's guess. Many will never find out. There will be lots of people who will insist on riding the No. 2 line only to find that their whole life was on the No. 4. As for me, I will, in accordance with my nature, ride each one.

[a continuation of 5 April letter to Ilona]

This morning snow is falling. Pouring down. And it's cold. Not at all extraordinary for April. Particularly not for an April after a winter without snow. Or at least without much snow. It will melt quickly. And, I hope, it won't harm our cherry tree, which is in blossom.

For the last two days I've been making an effort to collect my impressions of the last two years. Images keep popping up from the beginning of the war. Do you remember the empty streets of the seventh of April '92? The day Nedžad drove us to Grandma's?

Do you remember how flabbergasted our neighbours from Radičević Street were when we asked them, as soon as we'd arrived, what their basement was like and whether they would show it to us? Funny, on that seventh of April '92, the war had not yet begun for them in earnest for the sole reason that up to that point not one bomb had landed in their back yard. But we, we who lived only a twenty-minute walk farther on, already had under our belts the experience of forty hours spent in a chilly basement, filled to overflowing with neighbours, from babies to seventy-year-olds. But that first encounter with a bomb shelter was a mere lark compared to what was coming. And what was coming was the basement on Radičević Street, cold, damp, filthy, with a smell of sewage that made you gag, with mice that scurried underfoot, and the flickering candlelight, and the sleeping on old trunks and crates. And of course, the pounding of mortar shells on the building and around it. And the deliberate counting of the steps as we ran down from the fifth floor through the murky darkness: eight – five – eight – five. ...

My first impression of the war is written on the first page of the diary. There is no date:

"It's war! War. War. WAR. War in Sarajevo. Machine-gun fire, mortar shells. Death. Basement. Pillows against the windows. Dressers against the windows. Drawn blinds. Terror. Grief. Anticipation. Anxiety. Disappointment. Resignation. Misery. Humiliation. Fleeing. Weeping. Nerves. Humiliation. Humiliation. Humiliation!"

When I read that now, it strikes me as infinitely pathetic and contrived.

As though I'd chosen my words for effect. At the time it was probably the truth. A heap of feelings piled up between my stomach and my throat that needed to be released somehow. And I do it with words. I don't complain, I don't cry, I don't get depressed. I simply write.

I used up 281 pages in eight months. After eight months I no longer had either the will or the need to keep writing.

I recall, too, the time when something snapped inside me and I would no longer go down to the basement, or else I'd go merely out of solidarity. I'd go to work under shelling, come back amid "the odd bomb here and there" that was falling in front of me and behind me, and then head off to the basement for a good two-hour nap. While outside, all was quiet.

The snow has stopped falling.

Ciao! Love you.

THE TIMES OF LONDON, APRIL 15, 1994

Bosnian Serbs abduct Canadian peacekeepers

13 April 1994

This peace is a bald-faced lie. I don't believe in it now and I never did, not for one single second. But I've got used to it. Already. Please God, may I be wrong.

Once again today sniper's shots rang out across Marijin Dvor. And once again bombs fell somewhere. I heard them. On our positions, they say. All they need to do is overshoot a little for me to start sympathizing once again with the inhabitants of Goražde.

The Republic of Serbia captured UNPROFOR. Serves them right! You bet! When all they do is parade around with their fancy toys, their tanks and armoured personnel carriers. Well, now they've captured their tanks and APCs.

The snipers are back on duty. The city is once again blockaded, probably more thoroughly than a week ago – the airport is closed, the tunnel is closed, food isn't coming either by air or by land. And there you have it. ...

The "Čete" *["companies" of Serbian irregulars, the infamous Chetniks]* have imprisoned 155 UNPROFOR soldiers and 11 French humanitarian aid workers. "It takes balls to fuck over the whole world," someone will say. But *nyet, nyet* ... that's not the point. More to the point, it isn't much of a world. Fuck five billion people who can be checkmated by twelve million. Who don't even have an atomic bomb. As far as I know. Well, in fact, I did forget our dear former USSR, that is to say, "little mother" Russia. But don't let me get started on global politics. I'll get carried away jabbering about how Serbia's been forever sucking up to Russia and how Russia, in turn – maybe the good Lord and a historian or two know exactly from which date – has been forming an Eastern Orthodox axis. If that's where the problem is at all. But if it is, there extends towards us from the West a western axis, and we are, as usual, here somewhere – at their intersection.

So, how much longer until World War III? It's kind of scary: what if the shit hits the fan again here and the bombs start filling up the streets of Sarajevo with new death notices? My name might well show up on their list before I see the beginning of this latest world festival. And that would be a real shame. When I've already made it this far. It's as simple as this: I don't like it, in fact I can't stand it, when the power goes off in the middle of a movie. No matter how lousy it is. ...

17 July 1994

Dear Vesna,

I was in Zagreb! [...] After two years, I got out of Sarajevo! I latched onto the "normal" world! I saw Ilona!

My sister is going off to Australia. I came from Sarajevo to see her before she journeys off to the ends of the earth. Does this sound pathetic to you? Unfortunately, our lives have become too simplistic, and metaphors, both good and bad ones, have lost their raison d'être, for when I say that

160

Ilona is going to the ends of the earth, that's the plain truth – Australia, for me, is exactly that. Yes, it's unlikely that I'll ever make it there, and not because it is particularly far away from Sarajevo, but because everything is dreadfully far away from Sarajevo. Or more to the point, Sarajevo is far, far away from any point on this tragicomic globe, so far, in fact, from the life that we – that even I, through inertia – consider normal, that it would be necessary, in order for me to arrive anywhere, for me to stop being me. Hence, the problem is not a geographical one but a psychological one, and who knows, one day it may be a psychiatric one.

Look here, I have never believed that a person should spend his or her entire life in one place. On the contrary, I think you should change your residence as well as your job, and even your line of work, to the extent, of course, that you are in a position to do so. […] Now those are the kinds of changes I consider good, but the ones that are necessitated by a grievous reality, those changes alter our nature and render our soul not broader and more fulfilled, but rather mistrustful, wary, insensitive as much to others as to ourselves, and we quite simply cease being ourselves without being aware that this is happening. And, in fact, we end up dying in a sign of the horoscope different from the one in which we were born and in which we once long ago came to know ourselves for the first time.

I still struggle not to admit defeat and to put off surrender as long as possible – though I may have changed, I am sure that one of my traits has remained constant: stubbornness. It would have been an easy thing to stay in Zagreb once I had already arrived there, but the price of that freedom would be, for me in this moment, excessively high. Back in that prison was where I began the love story which is more precious to me than anything I could imagine. Over the past two years and some-odd months, I've been explaining to myself in various ways why it is I stay. […] There was always one common thread to all my attempts to understand myself: the need to explore the limits of my own capacity for endurance, which by itself implies a certain stubbornness and, naturally, curiosity. But seventeen days ago, I didn't return from "freedom" on that account, but rather for a much simpler, but therefore more acceptable reason: in Sarajevo, Pavle was waiting. And that's all.

That is in the end, a good and sufficient reason. Nevertheless, while I was sitting in the transport plane […] I was wondering what was awaiting me there, what I would feel when I once again […] met up with civilization, my sister, acquaintances, etc. Would I feel the urge to stay? Would I, in the encounter with the city, with the hubbub of the streets, with the people, cafés, movie houses, and theatres, forget Sarajevo? Perhaps all memory of Sarajevo would simply fade away.

The first striking feature for me was the traffic! […] I felt as though I had left the Sarajevo of 1900 and after an hour's journey arrived in the Zagreb of 1994. I was ashamed and humiliated – for the first time in my life I understood the frustration of a provincial. But the streetlights were working without the slightest glitch, crowds of people were waiting at the streetcar stops, walking down the streets, entering the shops, the advertisements were blaring…. Listen, you probably heard that these last few months, after the tragedy in Markale market, life in Sarajevo has started to become recognizably "urban." I mean, the streetcars have started up again, the so-called "blue roads" *[UN access roads]* have been opened so that large quantities of merchandise have begun reaching the city, prices have been falling precipitously, the situation with water and electricity is vastly improved, stores are opening, and cafés are springing up, both old and new. […] *[But]* for the citizens *[of Sarajevo]* all these ordinary things are still novelties, they're still a surprise and a source of pride: to put it simply, we notice them. The inhabitants of Zagreb aren't aware of these attainments of civilization at all. And it was precisely this absence of any acknowledgement of things that provoked in me various sorts of reactions that were astonishing, or more accurately, shocking!

I'd be lying if I asserted that nothing could attract the attention of passers-by, but […] they were intrigued by a sight that would have entirely escaped my notice in Sarajevo: they turned to look, albeit discreetly, at a figure in a bulletproof vest and with a light blue UN helmet, that is, at me. […] For me, there's nothing more normal than a member of UNPROFOR or UNHCR, or else some reporter in Sarajevo for the first time who, terrified by the thought of everything that could happen to him, tries to minimize the risk by walking around accoutred in this way. See, there's one more difference between me and a citizen of Zagreb.

Now it's time, I should think, to ask if you know the story of my letters and my book. [...] On the eighteenth of August, 1993 [...], I walked into the radio station of the Jewish Community Centre, Ilona turned towards me, and with her eyes on me, she said into the microphone, "Listen, Caka, my sister has just come in, it's her birthday today, and since you're about the same age, you should get to know each other." I came up, took the microphone, said hello to Caka, and we began to converse. And naturally, the two of us discovered that it was a total fluke that we didn't already know each other since we used to go out to the same places, we're the same age, we even had friends in common.... Caka wished me a happy birthday and begged me to write her a letter because she "lived off letters from Sarajevo." You see, Caka and her daughter had left Sarajevo in December of '92, and at that time she was living in Zagreb, working at the JCC radio station and waiting for her husband to get out of Sarajevo so they could go abroad together. Her mother was in Sarajevo, but her sister Adica was also in Zagreb along with *her* daughter, also waiting for her husband to come from Sarajevo.

I sat down and wrote Caka a letter. It travelled the way mail did in those days – as it still does – along with some journalist or someone from the JCC who had to, or was able to, go on business away from our prison. After maybe two weeks [...] I got a message saying: "I have never read a lovelier letter. I'm asking permission to have it published." The message was, of course, from Caka. I replied that as far as I was concerned, the letter could be published, provided anyone was willing to print it. And for me, that delightful compliment ended then and there.

She and her sister Adica typed out my letter, photocopied it, and passed it around to people who were interested in what was happening in Sarajevo. Adica translated it, and to make a long story short – it came into the possession of a reporter who published it in a Swedish newspaper!

Several months later, I received a huge parcel from Zagreb full of everything imaginable: honey, tea, baking powder, soup mix, garlic, coffee, spices, soap, deodorant, lighters, toothbrush, thick woollen socks, chocolate, and to top it all off: a notepad, paper and a pen for writing letters!

163

Those were all things that in Sarajevo were worth their weight in gold, and they were collected and sent by the people who had read my letters. There were seven donors!

What else can I tell you, except that Caka set off an avalanche – letters were published in various newspapers on various continents [...] I must also tell you that Ilona, who had in the meantime arrived in Zagreb, took over the work of organizing (Caka left for Prague along with her husband and daughter at the beginning of '94) and began putting together a book. The book should be coming out in September or October, and in it will be letters to Caka, Dunja, Adica, Ilona, and the Jelićes. One more little detail: it was quite a task in itself to collect all the letters, type them up, photocopy them and send them to me so that I too would have a copy of my own manuscript, because obviously, I hadn't written the letters in duplicate!

So, there you have the story of how your cousin became an "authoress."

THE NEW YORK TIMES, JULY 18, 1994

More 'Ethnic Cleansing' by Serbs Is Reported in Bosnia

18 July 1994

[a continuation of the 17 July letter to her cousin Vesna]
The first working day of this week. Today there's absolutely nothing to do and I'm bored. [...] Anyhow, I find it hard to be cooped up in an office from 8:30 to 4:30, surrounded by paperwork and telephones, giving out and finding information, etc., etc. After all, I used to be a teacher in a secondary school *["middle school," a kind of business college]*, and I was extraordinarily fond of that job. I loved the students, and to my great delight, they loved me. And they were satisfied with my lectures and in general with my rapport with them. But whom would I now teach philosophy? In other words: what would I say to the young people who no doubt believe that they have already learned in the course of this war everything they need to know about philosophy?

Anyhow, these young people, these students, are different from the ones that I used to teach, and who knows if we would be able to understand each other. And in the end, do I even believe that it is important and that it makes sense to teach philosophy to anyone?

All in all, this job that I have now at least pays very well, extraordinarily well, in fact, by Sarajevo standards. I get paid in German marks, and my salary is a hundred – now look, I'm not speaking figuratively, I'm giving you the bare facts – anyway, my salary is one hundred (100) times greater than my mother's or my father's. That is, as a secretary for a British humanitarian organization under the umbrella of the UNHCR, called Marie Stopes International, I earn one hundred times more than my mother, who continues to teach German and English in high school, and my father, who continues to work as a physician, and both of them have a good thirty years of work experience behind them. I get 500 DM and they get 5 each.

I was intending to describe to you some further incidents in the free world. [...] I had so much been looking forward to my first "outing" and shopping spree at a fine perfume shop! In the end, when I found myself in one [...] I didn't know what to look for, how to act, what I wanted, and even what there was to be had in such a store. Do you believe me? Well, if it weren't for the sickening sense of panic which seized me in that shop and which I feel even today when I remember the whole experience, I wouldn't believe it myself: all those glass cases with lovely boxes and bottles, with lipsticks and nail polishes, creams ... ah, I'm making an idiot of myself even now listing, like a child, all the colourful baubles that reduced me to confusion! I stood in the middle of that elegant cosmetics shop, surrounded mostly by elegantly dressed and made-up women who [...] appeared very relaxed, in contrast to me, who, despite having a slip of paper with an exact list of what I needed, didn't know what to look for. I had quite simply forgotten how it's done: how to buy and choose, how just to look around and ask questions without any intention of buying anything. Not even the salesladies paid any attention to me. Ilona was with me, but she couldn't help me – how could she when I myself had no idea what I was doing there? A real panic started to come over me – I knew I was supposed to look for something, buy it, but how? A saviour appeared in the form of one of Mom's friends whom I recognized and greeted. The woman was surprised and caught off guard and didn't know what to say, and in the end, like so many other people that I met, she began somehow to comfort me, of course, not because she had noticed my confusion, but purely and simply because I am from Sarajevo. Now this requires some explanation: luckily for me, I did not come across people who were unpleasant to me, although that is not a rare occurrence where newcomers from Bosnia are concerned. I experienced a different type of discomfort – when people realize where you come from they feel the need somehow to do you some sort of favour. The first feeling that they experience is sympathy and a need to comfort you. That isn't an attempt to understand, nor is it an effort to imagine or to listen to you; it's simply the consciousness, implanted in every human being, that one must have sympathy for those who suffer and that it is necessary to express this feeling in some fashion. This entire mechanism is subconscious and the person who is good by obedience to convention invests the minimum possible effort, and that means the minimum that won't inconvenience him or her, to display his or her goodness. Here arises sympathy, as the emotion that demands the least possible mental engagement, and after that comes "consolation" as the only thing that the one who pities you can do for you. That consolation amused me, and in fact, I started to feel bad about having involved that woman in a situation so uncomfortable that she didn't know what to say nor how to behave towards me. In the end I started to feel embarrassed by her behaviour, and I tell you, I don't know how I finally got out of that dreadful place.

1 August 1994

[conclusion to 17 July letter]
How long this illusion of peace will last I don't know, but I know that I'm not the only one who, like a bird of ill omen, is expecting a new outbreak of horror. A little while ago I was out with some friends from Eagleton's headquarters (they're concerned with the eventual revitalization of the city and the amelioration of immediate conditions – improving the supply of

water and gas and so on). One of them, whose name escapes me – all I know is that he was a Canadian – said that he was expecting a new escalation in the conflict in November or December of this year and that it might be worse than it had been. I asked him where this shit might hit the fan, and he replied: "In Sarajevo too." We shall see what we shall see.

As for me – I'm getting ready to get married! Are you still standing? Do you need water or sugar? Have you recovered? Fine, then I'll continue. Yes, I'm getting married to Mister Pavle Kaunitz. We're planning to tie the knot at the beginning of September. [...] The inspiration has come rather late to us, so we want to get an early start on it. Pavle happens to be a journalist, he's forty-four years old (eleven years older than I am, eleven centimetres taller and eleven kilograms heavier), he's fair-haired, with a ponytail, moustache, and beard. He was born in Sarajevo by his parents' choice (they were living in Zagreb, and his mother still is), and so he acquired BiH citizenship (which is really an enviable commodity these days), and then, again by his parents' choice, he spent the first half of his life in Zagreb, and then, at his own whim, he came to live in Sarajevo. To my great good fortune, because I doubt that we would have succeeded in meeting so fatefully and so happily anywhere else. Mind you, like the majority of people in love, we think we were bound to find each other, irrespective of trivial external circumstances and laughable details like space and time; and as the days pass, so we become more and more certain that, though other people may be deluded in giving themselves over to such ideas, in our case it is no illusion, but instead, the working of pure and authentic destiny.

10 September 1994

Dear Ilona,

Where are you now? By my reckoning – somewhere in the air, still above Europe.

My darling!

I'm flustered. I bumble, I stutter. I want to tell you something, masses of things, but somehow I just can't put them into words.

167

Tasmania is far away, so very far away. From here, everything is so very far away. Still – Tasmania!

I miss you, I miss you terribly. [...] Do you remember, I was in the habit of recounting to you everything that happened before that first panic-stricken dash into the basement on account of the mortar shells that were beginning to fall around us? In the course of two years of war, it all became somehow distant and vague, and I was afraid that in time I would remember nothing more of that "golden age." The past has faded frighteningly.

And then came this tenth of September, strange, this tenth day of the ninth month of the year 1994, for today everything came back. And it was painful. Cruel, the clarity of the images which began to emerge into consciousness; painful, the awareness of how good things were; it hurt, the realization that all that was gone and that now and forever, all those wonderful years are only a memory. What hit me hardest was the fact that I myself have changed so much that in the autobiographical film which was playing in my mind I had the greatest difficulty recognizing myself.

And all this started with a cassette [...] that Pavle had put on in the morning while I was waking up: we were lying in bed, I started to hum along and – I burst into tears. [...] I was singing, the tears were streaming down, at the refrains I would start sobbing ... and that went on until the afternoon. Sometime around six in the evening I finally fell asleep, and now I'm up, writing to you.

Today, today I became aware of the passage of time. And I realized that I have a past. From today my path has begun its descent. Actually, only now is it clear to me what memory is. It is a longing for beauty.

To think that you, in a way, have stayed behind in that past. You are a part of my memories: at least until the next time we meet. But you are so dreadfully, dreadfully far away and so dreadfully long ago.

19 September 1994

Dear Sis,

Today I'm feeling much better and so this letter will be painted with a brighter palette. How many days left until my wedding? Only five! So

168

you can imagine, I'm in quite a state. In truth, I'm most worried about my maid *[or matron]* of honour. [...] If she doesn't arrive in time (right now she's on business in Germany), we'll find someone else. As for Danilo *[the best man]*, he's promised not to budge from here, but all the same, I asked him sweetly to let me hold onto his blue card *[his UNHCR employee card, which gives him travel privileges denied ordinary Sarajevans]* until the wedding is over. After that, he can go where he pleases.

We spent a long time figuring out how we would organize everything, and in the end we decided to have a little reception [...] at the home of Pavle's Aunt Heda. [...] Mom and Heda are in charge of that part of the celebration, and I've given them *carte blanche* to come up with whatever they wish and, of course, whatever they can. How much they'll be able to do, I don't know, given that while we were waiting for the wedding party to be assembled in one place, the situation has again deteriorated. And I mean buggered up. Once again, no electricity, no water, no gas, and it's been like that for days already. I keep hoping that it will all be back on by Saturday, but really, I know it won't. But I'm not going to worry about it: after all, what kind of wartime wedding would it be if everything went just so?

As for the wedding dress [...], well, I'll be an entirely unconventional bride: I'll have a dark blue, almost black, very narrow skirt, a front and back insert with a high collar and long narrow sleeves of plum-coloured lace. The dark fabric is a very fine thin taffeta which falls beautifully, and the lace is from Mom's old dress. To go with it, my navy high-heeled shoes, dark stockings, and I'll probably have a long narrow low-cut jacket made from the same material. [...] Today I tried it on and it really will all look lovely – very formal and, for a bride, very unusual.

I asked the very nice ladies from the salon to whose ministrations I have entrusted myself for that day whether they would be able to finish sewing everything even if the power doesn't come back on, but they assured me that I didn't need to worry.

As far as hairstyling is concerned, obviously, it's going to be hard to do anything impressive with this shorn-sheep look of mine. Never mind – Pavle and I will be an extremely "well-balanced" pair: him with a ponytail halfway down his back, and me with a centimetre of hair covering my skull. Fabulous!

22 September 1994

[a continuation of the 10 September letter to Ilona]

The wedding is on Saturday at one o'clock, in the afternoon, of course. The blue roads are closed. Prices have almost doubled – which is to say that some absolutely essential items are already unavailable, e.g., chickens, and that Mom has moved heaven and earth to find them, and she did find them (at an astronomical price). The two of us have already spent more money than we had, which is to say that we're in debt – we haven't got married yet and we're already in the red! Not bad, I actually like the idea. As it happens, it just confirms the wise saying of someone with experience in the matter: "Marriage is the institution in which two people jointly resolve problems which they wouldn't even have if they hadn't got married."

There's no water, so Zoka hauled up fifty litres for me yesterday and another fifty today. [...] He's the new driver at MSI *[Marie Stopes International]*. [...] I have to say that MSI have really gone out of their way to help us – not just with water, but they've also lent us a car [...], and Debora prevailed upon her friend from the UNHCR to bring me walnuts from Kiseljak. Naturally, the man didn't make a special trip to Kiseljak for my walnuts, he was already there on business. He really was very sweet and brought me a whole kilogram – of peanuts! Crossed wires – I said I needed "nuts," but didn't say what kind, and so he brought me "pea." From this detail it can be concluded that there were no walnuts in the whole of Sarajevo. And also that the wedding cake won't have any. How that cake is going to be baked, I have no idea, except that I know that it's going to be extremely difficult to do it in our good old woodstove whose oven has never been the best, especially when the fuel is paper and cardboard!

Is this tale starting to sound familiar to you yet? I mean: "there's none of this," "none of that." It's a wonder "prosperity" and "peace" have lasted as long as they have. Granted, bombs have not started falling yet, not in Sarajevo, but in Bosnia as a whole, the war has not stopped.

170

Once again I have to come back to this fucking war. Fuck it! I can't seem to go for one single second without thinking about it. Not even while I'm rejoicing at the thought of my own wedding. But never mind, here's what just occurred to me: [...] It seems to me as though the period of savage killing (and here I'm speaking about Sarajevo) is at an end and that we're now entering a "warm/cold" phase, that is to say, things will get a little better, and then somewhere, one side or the other will attack, capture something, kill someone, and then there'll be a period of unrest – the occasional bomb will fall and the occasional person will be killed by a sniper. There will be terms and conditions: We won't let you have gas until you do such and such ..., if you want electricity, we want – I don't know what. Then there will be negotiations ad infinitum. Everyone will make deals but no one will be satisfied. Then a new turn for the better, while both sides regroup, and then more slaughter until they exhaust themselves, and so on, without end.

But we have decided to have a child. And as soon as possible. Whereas a year ago, I considered that such an act required more courage than I have, now I think I have even less time than courage. And we genuinely want a child.

The one thing I'm still not sure about is whether to stay here or to leave. When I think about staying, it seems to me I don't have anywhere to stay – this city of mine is changing too fast and too radically, and I'm afraid that the ultimate result of these changes won't appeal to me. If we stay here, it looks to me as though I will end up in a completely unfamiliar world, in a society whose customs I don't know, among entirely alien people. [...] Truly it terrifies me to think that I may, by choosing to stay here, find myself in a foreign land. In an enemy land. In a very new world in which there will be no place for me.

That is why I would actually prefer to leave. In that case I will at least understand why I don't feel at ease in that somewhere else, why people don't notice me or don't like me, why I can't realize my dreams and wishes. If nothing else, I'll have a justification for failure: I didn't make it in an alien environment. But how will I be able to justify my failures in the city in which I was born and where I was happy and contented for a good thirty years? And not just thirty, but thirty-three, because as you know, in the course of this war I have indeed been afraid, I have been disappointed, and I have felt betrayed, but I was not dissatisfied with myself, nor did I consider myself unfortunate as a result of what was happening – that is to say, I didn't perceive it as a personal misfortune, but rather as a social cataclysm which it was my duty to survive with the level of dignity that was expected of me.

Simply put – I don't fear the war, I fear the peace that will succeed it (on condition, of course, that I live to see it). I fear intolerance, primitivism, and ignorance. It will be the way it is after every revolution – the rule of the strongest, not the wisest. For me and for Pavle, that period will last too long.

2 October 1994

[a continuation of the 10 September letter]

How long have I been married so far? A whole eight days! I'm having a great time – if I'd known it was going to be this good, I would have done it sooner. Hey, hey, I bet you're waiting impatiently for my report. Naturally.

At the beauty salon there was no water and no electricity; and several of the hairdressers stared at me in amazement when I told them I wanted them to style my inch-long hair. In the end, the result wasn't bad.

Mom and Dad were already waiting for us in front of the city hall. Handsome, formally dressed, and excited. The other guests arrived only a minute later. And I can say that everyone was very sweet and in an excellent mood – all of us, nine in total. It was a gorgeous day, we were laughing and making all kinds of jokes, the windows of the municipal building were crammed with curious onlookers, at our backs stood Mt. Trebević, blue-grey, and I knew that there, too, through the other end of a sniper's scope, someone was watching us. Well, let them!

When it came time, we all filed inside, all of us except for Mom and Dad – they say that according to some custom, the parents shouldn't attend the actual wedding ceremony, because, apparently, it brings bad luck! Who knows what the real reason is, but I think the symbolic significance must be that finally, the time has arrived for two people to do something serious, to make an important decision without the advice or pressure, the persuasion or the presence of their parents. Only symbolically, perhaps, but you must admit it sounds just right – rather like: "You made your bed, now lie in it." *[lit.: "He fell himself; he killed himself."]*

The justice of the peace was on the third floor. A pleasant fellow received us, ushered us in through a glass door, and then not only shut it, but locked it, behind us! So if anyone had the least thought of backing out now, it was obviously no longer an option.

When I looked around me I saw:

1) a ladder; 2) a can of paint; 3) sitting on the paint can, a painter who was smoking and looking blankly right through us; 4) beside him, on the floor, paintbrushes.

Well, the picture was certainly comic – we were to be married not by a rabbi, nor by a justice of the peace, but by – a house painter! The two of us looked at each other and started to laugh – what else could we do? When I took a better look I saw that the room had been seriously damaged: a hole made by a mortar shell near the window had already been patched up, but there was a lot of shrapnel damage, the *de rigueur* plastic sheeting on the windows, an old, heavily damaged office table, a carpet rolled up in the middle of the room, stains, and huge ones at that, left by moisture on the walls – in one place you could see that water had been literally pouring down from the ceiling! I had to choke back my tears, because after the initial comic effect of the scene, the next impression was an eloquent reminder of the misery which, even though it did not exist within us, was nevertheless all around us. As surely as the splendid weather and the guests in their finery and the two, no, make that three cars that delivered the guests and the magnificent flowers intended for me succeeded in erasing the war from my consciousness, this room brought it back, and it struck me in the very midst of my happiness with so ruthless a blow that sorrow and disappointment filled even the most secluded parts of my being.

Luckily, the door at the far end of the room was opened, and there appeared before us an utterly delightful room, attractively furnished, with a carpet, a lovely large old-fashioned writing desk, with four chairs in front of it – for the bride, the groom, and the two witnesses – and two behind it, for the justice of the peace and the registrar. Granted, here, too, the large window had, instead of a pane, plastic sheeting, but that was more or less tolerable. In we went, and Pavle and I, Zehra and Danilo sat down, while the others stood behind us. In came Madame Justice of the Peace and a municipal employee, they greeted us, and the wedding ceremony began.

You know how it goes, nothing has changed, unfortunately. They still read the dos and don'ts of married life, etc., etc., and then comes the part: Do you, Elma Softić, consent to ... and, with a firm voice, I declared YES! Then the same question was directed to my dearest: "Do you, Pavle Kaunitz ...," and he answered: "Well, all right, sure."

Now imagine saying such a thing, for heaven's sake! The justice of the peace gave him a look, concluded that what he uttered was equivalent to a yes, and pronounced us man and wife.

Congratulations, kisses, flowers, gifts.

When we started down the stairs, the two of us in front, they started showering us with confetti. You know what, there was so much confetti that the whole staircase from the third floor to the ground floor was covered with it, as was the pavement in front of the entrance, not to mention the two of us.

24 November 1994

Dear Ilona!

Let's begin at the beginning. On Saturday, November 19, 1994, D. and Zoka (our driver [...]) came to pick me up to take me to the PTT building (that's the head office of UNPROFOR), because according to the new rules, personnel may travel to the airport only in armoured vehicles, but our car is an ordinary "soft" one. D. was going to Zagreb for the weekend, and I had to first go on company business to Split, and then to Zagreb on private business, namely, to the book launch of *[the Croatian edition of] Sarajevo Days, Sarajevo Nights*, so we had to "catch" an armoured personnel carrier that serves as a taxi between Sarajevo and the airport, via Dobrinja.

However, D. cancelled her trip at the last moment because the security situation was extremely precarious – we were expecting NATO air strikes on Chetnik positions in the *[breakaway]* Serb Republic of Krajina *[in Croatia]* from which the aircraft were flying that were bombing Bihać *[the UN-declared "safe haven" in northwest Bosnia]* with, among other things, napalm bombs. In the event of air strikes, the airport would be closed, likely for four or five days or more, and she had to be back in Sarajevo by Monday. Because she wouldn't be travelling herself, she decided that she would be the one, exclusively for the sake of my safety, as she put it, to drive me – through the Chetnik barricades on Kasindo Street, because for that route it wasn't necessary to have an armoured vehicle.

To be honest, I found it strange that she insisted on going that route, precisely because of the appalling tension in the air those days – after all, about ten days earlier, some of the "locals" had run into trouble at that checkpoint. Hence the recommendation to use the Dobrinja route, because that crossing point is controlled by the Bosnian army, which never makes trouble by, for example, holding up vehicles or searching or arresting passengers. Quite frankly, I did not relish the prospect of crossing a Chetnik checkpoint with a name like mine. However, I concluded that D. undoubtedly knew what she was doing, after all, she had always been concerned, even excessively, with our safety, so I simply said okay.

On the traffic cloverleaf at Stup, she asked me whether I had any mail, and if so, could I put it inside my bulletproof vest! By now I was starting to have a bad feeling about this. She knew very well that I was carrying with me at least two dozen letters – she was there when my colleagues at the office were giving me their letters, not to mention the people who used to come in with mail to be taken out by the first person to leave Sarajevo. Besides, she knew that I was carrying material on business – poetry by Sarajevo women which was supposed to be included in an anthology (that was the point of my travelling to Split) as well as papers, materials and the like, connected with my book.

At this point, at Stup, there was no longer anything to be done about it – not that it was impossible to stop, but it wouldn't have been good for our health even to slow down, given that a sniper and the "sower of death" were always shooting there, especially in the last little while, and particularly at white UNPROFOR and UNHCR vehicles. [...] Her question and suggestion, at that time and place, would have been quite funny, except for the fact that when you're passing that way, you ram your helmet down to your eyes, you slide down in your seat, your driver slams on the gas, and you pray to God for a clean miss!

From that moment on all I could think about was the fact that I was carrying with me not the twenty or so letters that D. could see, but at least three times that many.

There, at that checkpoint, they kept us for an hour and a half. In the beginning they weren't unpleasant, but as the time passed, they got more and more impatient, and by the end they had begun to behave in an entirely hostile manner. Things started to get complicated – they took all the material and the letters that they found (which weren't all the ones I was carrying) into a shack that housed the police station. D., who was visibly upset, went after them, and she later told me that they opened all the letters as well as a packet of photographs which I had been given by the mother of a fellow I'd taught with – photos from his childhood, remembrances of his late father, which I was supposed to give to his brother in Zagreb. [...] It was hilarious when D. told me, all pale, that they also opened a letter of hers in which she wrote to her parents that "Karadžić is a maniac"! Fun and games.

The silliest part of this whole unfortunate business with the letters was that I was carrying in the very same suitcase an opaque black bag full of letters from the JCC. And when they told me to open the suitcase and show them what was inside, I matter-of-factly, quite nonchalantly, took out this bag and placed it beside the suitcase! They didn't even look at it, and at first, I was pleased to have "put one over" on them, but later on, when things started to get messy, I just prayed to God that they wouldn't come and dig through everything all over again.

At first I stood beside the car and observed what was going on around me: various UNPROFOR and UNHCR vehicles were driving up, all of them were stopped and checked, some were searched, some people complained, the French doggedly wrote it all down – in general, no one else was held up the way we were, so the longer we waited, the more uncomfortable I got. Still, I did talk a little with the civilian police, a little with the military police, up until the time they moved off from me and started observing me from a distance. There were some comical situations, at least during the time that I was "on friendly relations" with the police of the Serb Republic *[of Bosnia]* – with the result that I even did some translating for them. I'm not kidding. Up comes an APC and a military policeman asks me what the name of that vehicle is. I say I don't know. He says "Ask her," pointing to D. I ask her, she answers, I translate. [...] I ended up translating a conversation between D. and the Serbian police, and naturally, I had some fun at her expense saying things like this: "Please, D., don't tell anyone that at Checkpoint Sierra 4 I was employed as a translator for the Serbian side – no one will believe that I'm doing this for free, and they might try me (and sentence me) as a Serbian mercenary." My boss didn't see the humour in my jokes at all, so I soon stopped annoying her. Anyhow, soon I didn't feel like joking either.

A red VW Golf with blue police licence plates stopped in front of the shack [...] and a man and a woman got out. [...] D. hurried out of the shack, came up to me, and told me to get in the car. She got in too and said that [...] the Serbs were angry because the letters and other written material were full of nasty remarks about them (this was pure make-believe, at least in regards to what I had written), and that they were ordered to escort me to the police station in Ilidža for further investigations – in other words, from that moment on, I could have cheerfully considered myself arrested, although I didn't realize it yet! Then D. used a VHF channel on the car radio to inform the UNHCR of our situation, but as it happened, no one who could actually have done something was there at that moment – they were at a meeting, or something of the sort. However, we soon heard the "radio room" announcing that a UNHCR car had been stopped and two employees arrested at Checkpoint Sierra 4!

What can I say – it was most distressing to hear that two "UNHaCeRs"* had been arrested – those would be colleagues of ours, after all! It was

*"*Unhacerovci*" in the original.

even more distressing when I figured out, a whole minute later, that one of them was me!

A burly man with a thick black moustache [...] came out of the hut – [...] he was very angry and came towards us waving some paper or other. [...] He asked me how I could be employed at two places. He was undoubtedly certain that I was a reporter, but according to the rules, as an employee of the UNHCR, I'm not supposed to be involved with journalism. I tried to explain that [...] the fact that I had an article published six months earlier did not make me a journalist, nor was I working and being paid as one. [...] The entire conversation was being carried on through the closed window of our car, because D. didn't want to open it – actually, she had locked me in the car, thinking that was the best way of ensuring that they wouldn't take me away – as though they couldn't have broken into it. The guy kept on yelling, asking me ("accusing" is more like it) why I was writing such disgusting things about them, i.e., Serbs. And anyhow, he said, they knew "everything." So this was a show put on for the benefit of the policemen who were gathered round.

If you ask me how I felt when things got so sticky that it looked as though they might actually take me away to Ilidža – I don't know. I wasn't panicked, I can't even say that I felt any particular fear – the one thing I clearly remember is my effort to imagine what might happen to me in a Chetnik police station there. I tried to imagine them beating me – and I couldn't. It didn't seem likely. Next I tried to picture myself being raped, and that too seemed unlikely. Not because I didn't believe that such things happen, but because I'm one of those people who are certain, up to the last moment, that "something like that can't happen to them" – you know the line: not me ("Planes will crash, but not the ones I take"). The only thing I managed to visualize happening in the police station in Ilidža was hours and hours of exhausting interrogations. It didn't even occur to me that maybe they wouldn't even waste a minute on me, but might try to exchange me right away (as, apparently, happens these days) for *[a Chetnik POW in]* Bihać. So I could have found myself in the middle of the offensive in Bihać, without the slightest chance, at least for the moment, of getting back to Sarajevo.

The furious fellow went away, D. got out of the car again and came back a short time later. The guy with the moustache had said in a rage, how dare she bring along a Muslim woman as a translator. At this point I started to laugh, but D. warned me for the second time that this was no time for jokes. I explained that this was all total idiocy: first, I'm not a translator [...]; secondly, I don't know why a Muslim woman shouldn't be a translator, too, if her English is good – surely specific jobs aren't reserved for specific nations, e.g.: All translators are Serbs. All Serbs in a single state. Ergo, all translators in a single state. And finally, thirdly, I have never in my life thought of myself as a Muslim, even though I have always been proud of the fact that I am descended from fine Muslim forebears, among others. I suspect that D. didn't entirely follow my argument. Anyway, she asked me how "Muslim" my name was. I said, "Very," and realized that the old saying "Call me a pot, but don't break me" ought to go: "Don't break me, even if I'm called a pot."

D. got out of the car again and tried to get help from a French soldier [...], which is to say, she went to UNPROFOR for help. [...] The French were confused: they figured out that something was going on, they saw all the other cars passing through and only us held up, and big Mr. Whiskers was awfully annoyed about something and was bellowing like a bull elephant, but the poor fellows didn't understand a single word of Serbian, nor, it follows, of Croatian or of this newest language, Bosnian (it's still one and the same language, as far as I'm concerned), nor of English [...], and of course, they were unable to help us. Not that they would have been able to help us even if they understood every word of every language of the world, because UNPROFOR is nothing but a scam, a tiny little mouse, a teeny tiny one, the tiniest in the world – so tiny it doesn't dare poke its little snout out of its hole, not even while all the Chetniks in the world, including the ones in the Serb Republic, are sleeping the deep sleep of the utterly justified!

Perhaps two minutes after the unsuccessful attempt to mobilize the forces of protection of the United Nations, a tall, very handsome French soldier showed up (he was driving past). D. stopped him and took the whole story once more from the top. The man spoke perfect English! [...] Well, he listened calmly to D., then came to my window and asked, "Whatever possessed you to go through Sierra 4?"; two or three times he shook his head as if to say, "Tsk, what a silly fool..."; and he turned away. D. asked him if he could give us permission to leave, he said we should just leave, turned around, got into his car, and drove off. When D. finally got our car started, he was no longer anywhere in sight, and therefore, the assembled policemen of the Serb Republic who had been keeping a watchful eye on us the whole time started to jump up and down and wave their arms around, and one very young one, I think he was barely seventeen (or at least he looked it), fired off a round of bullets. We stopped the car.

At about the same time, it was announced over the radio that the head administrator of the UNHCR was on his way over and that we should wait calmly for him to arrive. Less than a minute after this announcement a military policeman came and ordered us to make ourselves scarce as soon as possible and in the general direction of the city.

What precisely happened, I don't know. I assume that the UNHCR chief was in radio contact with Sierra 4 and that he talked them into letting us go. In the end, they probably didn't think it worth their while to "lock horns" with the UNHCR, even though only two days later at the same checkpoint, two translators were arrested and taken away to Ilidža. I got off lightly!

When we finally arrived in front of the UNPROFOR headquarters, the head administrator was there waiting for us along with two other men.

They asked me if I still wanted to go to Split and why I was pale. I replied that I wasn't about to cancel my trip and that my pallor was due to the fact that I hadn't been to the "seaside" in four years. They put me in an armoured vehicle and drove me nicely, without any problems, past the Bosnian army checkpoint to the airport.

I was on the passenger list for flight number – I don't remember any more – departing at 12 noon. At 11:45 the passengers were informed that the flight was being cancelled and the airport closed because an American plane had been fired upon.

I was home by about 12:30, and Pavle and I went to the JCC for lunch. There I briefly recounted my adventure to Mom and Dad and anyone else who was interested. Around 3 p.m. we were back home. Pavle put some fuel in the stove, and I was suddenly seized with a chill. I barely managed to take off my boots, and fully dressed as I was (except that I'd removed my coat) I lay down and covered myself with a blanket. Even so I was cold, so I put on a thick sweater and Pavle brought me a second blanket, and two minutes later, a third. I continued to shake, I had a headache and felt nauseated. The fear that had been absent that morning caught up with me at last. Finally I fell asleep and woke up late in the evening, changed into my pyjamas and went to bed. I was determined to fly the next day, on the condition, of course, that the airport was open.

But the airport was closed Sunday morning [...] and it's closed today as well, until further notice.

All in all, I doubt I will succeed in getting away, and consequently – I won't be at the launch of my own book. And it's my first one. Of course, there's always the option of going on foot through the tunnel by Mt. Igman, but to be honest, I'm not in the mood for it, despite my adventurous nature. Actually, I think I have a good reason for not subjecting myself to what is, in the final analysis, an unnecessary stress; but I'll tell you about that some other time – once I'm certain.

7 December 1994

[conclusion of 24 November letter to Ilona]
I didn't make it to Zagreb – the airport was closed and still is today. And as for forcing myself to go through the tunnel and over Mt. Igman, in the snow, well, I didn't want to, or more to the point, I didn't dare to. And how is it that your hardy big sister lost her nerve all of a sudden? [...] My "good reason" is as follows (you'd better be sitting down for this): the reason has to do with the fact that you are going to be an aunt!

Lots of love,

Elma

A nervous week behind us. [...] The death of two French peacekeepers dismayed the world, and Monsieur François Léotard, Minister of Defence of the French Republic, came from France to attend their final *envoi* from Sarajevo.

The Chetniks claim that they were killed by the Bosnian army, i.e. the "Muslims," as they dub everyone on this side of the front. In fact, Karadžić goes on about the approximately forty thousand "captive" Serbs *[in Sarajevo]* who are being terrorized by the Muslims and suffering unspeakable reprisals, and whom the "mujaheddin" won't allow to cross into Serbian territory. Radovan thinks that these forty thousand can't wait to be resettled by him in far-flung villages or bombed-out towns, or else to be mobilized *[into the Bosnian Serb Army]* – no doubt they would far rather die on that side than on this. Every living Serb who is eligible for military service understands that if there ever was a time when he could cross over to Grbavica and make his way to Serbia (which for most meant Belgrade), today there's very little chance of that left.

According to our information services, the Chetniks are responsible for the murder of the Frenchmen. After all, the other day Karadžić publicly declared the UN forces to be enemies of the Serbian people.

A few days ago on Serbian TV, there was a report on the death of Maja Djokić, a seventeen-year-old Sarajevan who was killed ten days ago in the middle of Sarajevo by a mortar shell. The Serbian news agency SRNA announced:

"A Serb in Muslim-held Sarajevo, Maja Djokić, was captured during her attempt to flee to Serbian territory, and on the spot, the street, she was raped repeatedly and then killed, and her corpse left there. The perpetrators were, of course, Muslims. After the crime was committed...."

... along comes UNPROFOR and picks up the corpse. At the very same time, the Bosnia and Herzegovina Broadcasting Corporation is running a story on the shelling of the city and the casualties, dead and injured. Among them, Maja Djokić. She was of interest to our media as well: young, many-talented (she played piano, was on a volleyball or basketball team, I don't remember exactly), very popular among her peers, and so after her death, she was written up in a newspaper article, and there were interviews with her friends on TV. According to their testimony, Maja was coming back from her team practice that evening and was killed by a shell.

A death by mortar shell is such a logical thing in Sarajevo. There probably isn't a single inhabitant of this city who doesn't know someone who was killed in that fashion, or who perhaps was an eyewitness to such a death, or was wounded himself or herself. Not for a moment did I have any suspicions about the cause of Maja's death. But I was unnerved by the Serbian TV report, not so much by its monstrous claims, as by the fact that the majority of the people on that side believe it! Ordinary people who didn't want a war any more than I did, who don't understand the ideas and goals for which they're supposed to risk their lives. People who did not hate until someone taught them to. It's appalling to think that for them it as just as logical to assume that Maja died of the causes reported on their TV as it is for me to assume that the true explanation is – a mortar shell.

THE NEW YORK TIMES, MAY 25, 1995

NATO May Be Called On to Silence Guns in Sarajevo

By ROGER COHEN
ZAGREB, Croatia, May 24 — Responding to Sarajevo's steady slide back into terror and isolation, the United Nations commander in Bosnia and Herzegovina issued an ultimatum today threatening NATO air

25 May 1995

Dear Nada,

... You have to say something, call someone, utter one single word, and everything will be all right, everything will be cleared up and there will be an end to your torment. But however much you try, your mouth won't open, as though it's been sewn up tightly, glued shut. You strain and strain and panic takes hold of you and you feel as though the veins on your temples are popping, but still, no sound. Finally, finally, you feel your jaws moving apart, but instead of a scream, out from that gaping hollow comes – nothing but silence! You're mute as a corpse.

Well, that's how I feel – I keep trying to find a means of dispatching

183

this heap of paper to you, but frankly, I have no means at all.

See – I already have more than seventy pages, and that's a lot when you have to ask someone to deliver it. Especially since the airport has been closed for six-and-a-half weeks already, so that people either go by car through one of the checkpoints and aren't willing to carry even a letter along in case they run into some problems; or else they go through the tunnel under the runway, and once again, they don't want to take on the responsibility. Mind you, it's been a long time since anyone I know has gone out of the city, so I haven't even had the chance to ask anyone. Only once did the opportunity present itself, but the man who was going, a foreigner, didn't dare risk it in view of the highly precarious situation – I don't know what route he was taking, I think across a checkpoint, but he told me very nicely that he couldn't risk taking so much material, especially since he had no idea what it was about.

Faxing it to you is out of the question. That method would cost me at least 70 times 10 Deutschmarks (more, counting this letter), i.e. to send a page of text to Canada costs $10, and I don't have that kind of money.

Finally I found a friend who can send it by E-mail, but that has been quite time-consuming, given that the text had to be put onto a disc, and I don't have a computer at home, and anyhow, I'm not especially computer literate. So fine, I found a computer, but then other difficulties cropped – two days last week of bombardment so heavy that I didn't leave the house at all, and after that an afternoon of no electricity, then a weekend, when the office where I could enter the data was closed.

And to top it all off, yesterday's heavy bombardment of Sarajevo, so that not even Pavle, whom I had asked to help me, could leave the house, nor could I go to the place after work – I was lucky it eased up for an hour, long enough for me to get home.

So here I'm writing you this new letter today. A letter of apology, of self-justification, call it what you will.

Anyhow, although there is a general alert in effect, in my part of the city it's been very quiet since morning. Unpleasantly quiet. Tense. We're expecting something at any moment, so citizens have been advised to go outside as little as possible. There is such an atmosphere of menace that I

184

didn't go to work this morning. Today I am afraid. O God! But it's a gorgeous day. But I'm afraid, and from the time shells started falling on Sarajevo once more, I mean, after that year of calm (in a qualified sense), I am much more afraid than I was in the worst periods of '92 and '93. To be honest, I saw this coming. I knew that death was only lying in wait, that the calm was only a pause, I was careful not to relax too much, not to forget, but all the same, when it started up again, I was caught by surprise, unprepared, disappointed, and terrified. Crushed. And so are most of the people I meet.

Besides, now I have, in some sense, more reasons to be afraid. Listen, I'm in my eighth month of pregnancy [...] I'm no longer as quick on my feet, actually, I don't dare permit myself any sprinting across intersections, running away from explosions, not even any inattentive walking along the ripped up streets of Sarajevo. I'm horrified by the thought that I might be injured, that I might lose the baby. I'm revolted by the idea of having to go down into some sort of basement on account of the sickening bombardment, especially if it were to happen at a time when I wasn't at home, and that I would have to spend several hours or the whole day there, or else even spend the night.

This peace is killing me – I don't want to be a bird of ill omen, but this does not bode well.

I don't know how much and what and how your media are reporting about BiH, whether you get news from the battle zones or whether you get any information about UNPROFOR operations here. Well, you know that according to one of the agreements that was signed some time ago, all heavy weaponry in a zone of 20 km. around Sarajevo was supposed to have been put under UN control. And it was. Certainly not all of it, but in any case, UN forces at certain points were in control of heavy weaponry, which meant that it could not be employed under any circumstances. Such areas in which there are no heavy weapons are called "exclusion zones." Over the past month, attacks on Sarajevo and other exclusion zones have intensified, and the situation has particularly deteriorated in the past two weeks. Attacks on the so-called "control points" and seizures of heavy weapons have become more frequent. Let's be clear about this, the attacks

185

are being carried out by Chetniks *[i.e., Serbs]*, and so far quite a lot of artillery pieces have been taken back and are now firing on the city. Why am I explaining all this to you? Because yesterday I read in the paper a statement by the civilian spokesperson of UNPROFOR in connection with the seizure of weapons from one of the points in the vicinity of Sarajevo. I was standing in my office, the building was shaking from the explosions, and I was laughing like an idiot. Rather than repeat the whole statement, I'm sending you a photocopy of the newspaper article entitled, "Only One Howitzer Returned."

ONLY ONE HOWITZER RETURNED

Sarajevo, 23rd May (ONASA) According to an announcement by the civilian spokesperson of UNPROFOR in Sarajevo, Alexander Ivanko, Karadžić's Serbs this morning returned one of the two howitzers which they had seized yesterday from the UN control point for heavy weaponry at Poljine, "cleaned and polished."

According to this source, this is one of the reasons that leads UNPROFOR to suppose that Karadžić's Serbs seized the weapons "perhaps for maintenance purposes." Spokesperson Ivanko acknowledged that there might also be "other reasons" for the seizure of the weapons.

Karadžić's Serbs this morning returned a 105-mm. howitzer, but they kept a 122-mm. howitzer. Yesterday, before the seizure, they imprisoned 23 members of UNPROFOR in the UN observation tower at Poljine and released them only after the removal of the weapons.

I don't think any additional comment is necessary, but I must point out that there is a sequel to this news report: yesterday that same control point was attacked once more and the weaponry removed, probably permanently. This time UNPROFOR reacted somewhat more strongly: the commander of the UN forces in Bosnia-Herzegovina, General Smith, gave the Serb Republic *[of Bosnia]* an ultimatum and two deadlines:

1) that the stolen weapons be returned by noon today, that is to say, the twenty-fifth of May, and restored to UN control; failing which, Serbian positions around the city will be bombed; and

2) that the shelling of Sarajevo be stopped and that the heavy weaponry be placed under UNPROFOR control or else withdrawn from the exclusion zone [...], failing which Serbian positions around the city will be bombed.

Anyhow, after 12 noon, Smith announced that the artillery was not returned, and now we're awaiting the next move.

As to whether NATO will actually do any bombing, I refuse to speculate. The UN has to issue the command, but the UN has ended up looking ridiculous so many times by making threats it has not carried out and by avoiding any conclusive definition of the situation or of its own rule in this whole circus, by attempting to resolve the "conflict" "by peaceful means" long after BiH has buried hundreds of thousands of people, etc., etc. As a result, I no longer believe a single word from anyone who is in any way associated with the "international community."

It's still the twenty-fifth of May. Ten in the evening. NATO really did bombard a weapons depot near Pale, around 5 p.m.

Bodies blown to pieces, a leg torn off, bloodied tablecloths, a decapitated trunk, a bloody town square, 61 dead so far, around 200 injured, 30 of whom may not survive.

That's the toll from one mortar shell that landed a little before nine last night in Tuzla, in a square which was the usual gathering place of youth. There were about 2,000 of them – they say that not one of the slain victims was more than twenty-eight years old. Those killed were mostly high school and university students, but there happened to be three children as well. The eldest was four years old. Selected. The victims were selected.

And that evening, just after seven, a general alert had been sounded – shells were falling over the defending army's positions. The citizens of Tuzla have no experience of the Vaso Miskin *[Street breadline massacre]* or of the Markale *[market massacre]*. They paid no attention to

187

the warnings of the civil defence. Not even the mortar shell, the penultimate one that evening, which landed somewhere in the centre of town, was a sufficient warning.

And they had gone out to walk around, to meet their friends, to see their boyfriends and girlfriends. It was such a delightfully warm and mild evening, it was such a treat after the days of rain that had preceded it. You see, last night May finally decided to be May and to lure out the handsomest, the fittest, the most beloved, the merriest, the most gifted....

And they were selected. They were not "accidental victims."

It can't be an accident that in one immeasurably short moment so many of those of whom the most is expected and whom every enemy most fears are killed. It can't be an accident when at a single stroke so many of those whose death hurts the most are crushed.

Do you know what Gary Coward, a spokesperson for UNPROFOR, said? Mr. Coward said, "Not in my country, they're not showing these pictures!" ... The worst never happens here, never to us. God Almighty! Look, there in god-forsaken Tuzla, somewhere in savage Bosnia, some kind of cannibal tribe killed the children of some other cannibal tribe. That can't happen here. *We* are civilized.

... After all, who feels like watching those bloody scenes when you can flip through the TV guide and easily find a good selection of movies of that type. You'll get the satisfaction you're looking for, the lighting will be better, the frames will be clearer, the details will be more striking, the directing more professional.

And all this can go to the bunker. Anyhow, one day they'll make a film of this, too. That'll be much better – artistically produced, with a message, not this kind of raw material which does nothing but turn your stomach.

The world is hypocritical. And the worst thing is to look and not see.

Nada, have you read *The Picture of Dorian Gray*? Well, the world – the world is the picture of Dorian Gray. But at first glance, it seems perfection!

Yesterday NATO forces executed another air strike of military targets in the vicinity of Pale. Just as the reprisal for the first bombing was murder – according to the latest statistics that I heard on the radio, sixty-three victims (twenty-five are still fighting for life) – so the consequence of yesterday's strike was the disarming and capture of around 120 UNPRO-FOR soldiers, from various control points and from different nationalities – French, English, Ukrainians....

Some of these poor fellows were handcuffed to strategically important locations which the Chetniks consider may be the next targets of NATO bombers.

Blue Helmets, soldiers of the United Nations, hence, representatives of the world, tied to poles like dogs! The Serb Republic *[of Bosnia]* holds the world to ransom! And why shouldn't it – it gets away with it: That very world, up until now, hasn't shown signs of anything except a miserable impotence.

They say: The mandate of UNPROFOR is not to establish peace, to wage war, but rather to safeguard peace. What peace? Here there hasn't been any for three years. You can't guard a safe that doesn't exist. In the same way, you can't keep a peace when there isn't one.

UNPROFOR is, in point of fact, supposed to ensure the delivery of humanitarian aid – hence, to safeguard the UNHCR convoys that carry aid here. But it doesn't do even that – the airport has been closed for two months already, and food isn't coming in by land either, neither to Sarajevo nor to Bihać.

UNPROFOR has the right to defend itself if attacked. Well, then, how come at least 120 of them were captured and tied to stakes like village mutts?

Those poor sods are in Bosnia for one single reason: to ensure that the interested parties have a place in the arena of world politics. They're there in service of the great powers' settling of accounts. Just as this war is finally nothing but a chessboard for the grand masters of power.

Have you ever wondered why the UN, in one of its resolutions or declarations (let them call the document what they will), doesn't lift that shameful embargo on the import of arms to Bosnia-Herzegovina? First point: the prohibition on arms imports was never applied to Bosnia-Herzegovina, but rather on the former Yugoslavia. After Yugo fell apart (I have to say it again: "regrettably"), BiH was received into the United Nations as a full member. [...] But when the war in BiH started, in other

189

words, when Karadžić said loud and clear that all Serbs must live in one state [...], then the "Yugoslav National Army" (which long ago stopped being either Yugoslav or National) [...] threw itself completely behind the Serbian Democratic Party of Radovan Karadžić, and of course – packed up and took along all the weaponry, including what didn't even belong to it, namely, the weapons of the units of the civil defence.

And there you have it: well-armed units of renegades (it's obvious that not all the members of the "Yugoslav National Army," neither officers nor enlisted men, stayed to fight in Bosnia) with tanks, cannon, multi-barrel rocket launchers, etc., etc., (I don't know all the names for them) as well as huge quantities of infantry weapons and ammunition, on one side, and on the other side, the citizens of Bosnia-Herzegovina, on paper, sovereign, independent, and internationally recognized, with hardly any weapons at all!*

As you can see, the UN has never lifted from this Bosnia-Herzegovina the arms embargo which, as I said, was never meant to apply to this new state. The explanations for this run along the following lines: "lifting the arms embargo would lead to further conflicts and more bloodshed." That is, in the final analysis, correct: not only would the citizens of Bosnia be dying, but so would those others as well, but for God's sake – that's called "war." If we have to be exterminated, let it be in a fair fight and not like cattle herded for slaughter.

And once more, to repeat the question with which this whole "political analysis" began: why doesn't the UN lift the arms embargo?

Answer: Because in that case the interested powers would lose control of the situation. Then it would be just one more internal conflict between a government and rebels, a conflict in which no outside parties would have any right to get involved. Admittedly, there would be no help from the UNHCR either, but I imagine that people would be found who would be willing to sell food for a profit, just as other people are making a profit selling arms. But money, where would the money come from? Well, for

---

*According to an estimate submitted to the U.S. Congress in September 1992, the Bosnian Serb Army had 300 tanks, 200 APCs, 800 artillery pieces, and 40 aircraft. Government forces had two tanks and two APCs.

God's sake, you can't prevent anyone from donating their money to whomever they wish.

Nada, it's really not my style to lay on so much bullshit (pardon my language) about politics (again, pardon my language), but I can't stand to listen any longer to the moronic declarations of world leaders (that is to say, world-class bums) to the effect that "Radovan Karadžić's Serbs must be sternly warned," that "both warring parties must be brought to the negotiating table and the conflict resolved by peaceful means." Because leaving aside the slaughter in Tuzla, the attack on UN soldiers and everything that is going to happen in the future, it's unlikely that Mr. Boutros Boutros-Ghali is going to do anything other than what he has been doing all along: writing letters and giving warnings "to both sides" and that sort of thing. The UN will never give NATO the go-ahead for any larger-scale action. If you think that thought brings terror to my soul – you're wrong. I'm not crazy about the idea of American military intervention. I'd rather you give us those arms so we can finally put an end, one way or the other, to this horror show.

Actually, what interests me most is how this show will end. What will become of Bosnia? Will it survive as "multinational" and "multicultural" and multi-this, multi-that? I fear, I truly fear that there's not much of that "multi-" left. Three years is just too long a period for a splendid idea like that to exist. There's been too much evil perpetrated, too much nationalism, too many myths and legends, too many memories.

But enough of that. I'm tired of this business.

Love,

Elma

23 June 1995

Dear Nada!

You won't believe me – just now when I was putting down the date, first I was going to put '92. Ninety-two was when the war started. So then I wrote '94, then I corrected that to '96, and in the end I yanked out the sheet of paper and put in a new one. You see, I've completely lost all notion of

191

time. [...] Under the circumstances, it's not the least bit surprising that I can't keep my dates (or years) straight anymore. The way things are going, there will come a time when I'll be getting my decades mixed up, not just my years.

What more can I tell you about Sarajevo. The situation is appalling. We've run out of absolutely everything – starvation is advancing with ever surer giant's steps, and perhaps our only stroke of good fortune is the fact that we've moved into summer, so we'll have a few vegetables from the improvised balcony gardens or from the plots that have sprung up in the city parks. Of course, those obliged to buy them at the market will be spending whole fortunes for them – the price of all food has just soared. Yesterday potatoes were 6 DM per kilogram, but what's worse, the food vanishes before your eyes and it's simply impossible to find any to buy. Experience has already taught me that it is impossible to store up sufficient supplies of food – you can never have enough to outlast the hunger, whether it's because you don't have the money to buy it or whether there's nothing to buy (in May of '92 you could have offered a billion dollars for a kilogram of potatoes and still not have been able to buy any).

As for the rest, it hasn't got the least bit better – people are burning clothes to bake their bread (in a good oven one Adidas or Converse running shoe is enough for a loaf), and they haul water from the city fountains. But waiting at a water source is an act of brinksmanship – four days ago eight people were killed by a single shell as they stood in a queue for water. That's why two of us were collecting rainwater yesterday. Can you picture this scene: torrents of water from both heaven and earth, water streaming down the streets, and people running out with pots and pans of all shapes, sizes and purposes and setting them up under drainpipes riddled with shrapnel holes. And anyone lucky enough to "claim" one of the unoccupied pipes pouring water into the street to shove under it enough cans, tubs, barrels, pots, etc., etc. yesterday could have collected tens of litres in the wink of an eye. Luckily, this summer, that is to say, spring, has been extremely rainy. Yesterday, for example, Pavle collected and brought home the water, and I did the laundry, rinsed out my stockings, and cleaned the bath and toilet. To top it all off, I had a lovely bath in rainwater – the old people say that rainwater is a good conditioner for hair. We even managed to store a whole barrelful for the next few days. We don't actually drink rainwater, but we'll use it to wash our stuff and ourselves (mind you, we did chlorinate it, and chlorine we have, thank God, at least for the moment). We bring drinking water from one of the fountains, but we chlorinate it as well – enterocolitis and jaundice are once again on the increase.

I myself don't know how I am. The baby is due five weeks from now. I'm in good shape, I'm still working at the office, and I'm getting things ready for the baby. We haven't yet finished the biggest task – cleaning the apartment, especially the disgustingly dirty walls which, say the experts, there's no chance of cleaning up properly, given the unbelievable amount of soot that has built up over these years of war. […] I don't need to tell you that there is no paint to be had anywhere in the city, so we'll be using whitewash, which is probably even better because lime is a disinfectant. The only thing is, we'll have to haul hundreds of litres of water!

So, how am I – otherwise? I guess I'm somehow more afraid. The shelling scares me out of my wits. Gone are the days when I didn't even notice the explosions. Each one makes my nerves snap and drives ugly terror into every last one of my cells. I can't say that I've shut myself up in my apartment – I don't dare, because I believe that that's precisely the way madness lies – but I get the most awful feeling when I walk down the street, expecting a shell to land at any moment. Besides that, I'm worried about the birth itself – a few days ago, in the hospital, in their hospital beds, two people were killed, and even before that, a pregnant woman who was about to undergo a Caesarian section was wounded. In the stomach. By a stroke of luck and, no doubt, the mercy of God, both she and her child survived, and without serious injury. You know, anything can happen: for example, there could be so much shelling that I won't be able to get to the hospital. That's still much better than having some disaster happen in the hospital itself. I don't know how religious I am, but I do know that I am always thanking God that we have survived up till now, and I pray to Him to preserve us in the future as well. How do I do that – in the only way I know how, but He understands, they say, all languages.

[My colleagues] have left it up to me to decide whether or not to come to the office at all, depending on how dangerous it is (or at least, how dangerous it seems to me – there are no objective parameters for the quantity of danger which might descend at any given moment on the city as a whole or on any one square metre of it). All the same, I make a point of conforming with the majority of people in the city, and when the terror becomes too enormous ... well, then what, I don't know, I'll write you another letter.

Nada, I'm off. Ciao. Say hello to your parents and to everyone I know in Canada. Hugs and kisses.

Your

Elma

Translator's Guide to
Sarajevo Days, Sarajevo Nights

Text

The manuscript from which I worked was a compilation of (a) photo-copies of original letters; (b) photocopies of retyped versions of letters and diary entries (typing done by Elma and friends); (c) the Croatian book *Sarajevski Dani, Sarajevske Noći*; and (d) text downloaded from E-mail (the material from July 1994 on).

Given the sophistication and playfulness of Elma's prose style, the numerous local and topical references, slang, and other peculiarities of Sarajevan speech, and my own limitations, I would have found the task of translation impossible without the help of native speakers (thank you, Cynthia Ashperger!) and especially, of Sarajevans. I am deeply indebted to Emir Geljo and his wife Amira, Saša and Gordana Bukvić, and Boro and Aida Krneta (a.k.a. Adica) for helping me to understand not only the language but the spirit of Sarajevo. And, of course, Elma and her mother Sadrudina, patiently answering my questions and generously sharing their stories with me *de profundis*, have been a blessing and an inspiration.

Pronunciation

Serbo-Croatian (a.k.a. Bosnian) is spelled phonetically, but note the following:

c = "ts"; *ć* = soft "ch" (dental, like Dutch "tj"); *č* = hard "ch" (with the tongue farther back); *đ* or *dj* = soft "j"; *dž* = hard "j"; *j* = y; *š* = "sh"; *ž* =

"zh"; *a* as in "car"; *e* as in "ten"; *i* as in "see"; *o* as in "for"; *u* as in "moon."

Stress is usually recessive (i.e., towards the beginning of the word). Thus: *Alifakovac* = Ah'-lee-fah"-koh-vats; ˇCaršija = Char'-shee-yah; *Karadžić* = Kah'-rah-jeech; *Oslobođenje* = Oh'-sloh-boh-jen"-yeh.

I have generally followed the spelling of the original manuscript, but have used Anglicized versions of the better known names. Thus: "Belgrade" for *Beograd*; "Bosnia-Herzegovina" for *Bosna i* [=and] *Herzegovina*; "Chetniks" for *Četnici* [singular: *Četnik*]; "Sarajevans" for *Sarajlije* [masc.] and *Sarajke* [fem.] (both end in -*a* in the singular); "Ustashas" for *Ustaši* [sing.: *Ustaša*]; "Yugoslavia" for *Jugoslavija*.

Street names in S-C have genitive or adjectival endings. Thus, the full name of Tito Street is *Ulica Maršala Tita*, popularly shortened to *Titova Ulica*. Radičević Street is shortened to *Radićeva* (as though from Radić, instead of *Radičevićeva*) for obvious reasons.

Currency

The currency of the former Yugoslavia was the *dinar*. The government of Bosnia-Herzegovina issued state coupons after independence, but the unofficial currency remained the *Deutschmark*. As of June 1995, the German mark was roughly at par with the Canadian dollar and trading at about $0.72 (U.S).

Geography

Of the place names that occur in the book, the following refer to residential districts (for which the old Turkish word is *mahala*) and other localities in and around Sarajevo:
Alifakovac, Babića-bašta, Bačevo*, Baščaršija, Bistrik, Bjelave, Breka, Butmir*, Ciglane, Ćolin Potok, Dobrinja, Drvenija, Grbavica*, Hrasnica,

196

Hrasno, Hum, Ilidža*, Koševo, Kovači, Lukavica*, Mejtaš, Neđarići, Poljine*, Sedrenik, Širokača, Skenderija, Sokolović-kolonija, Soukbunar, Stup, Vasin-han, Vogošća*, Vratnik, Vrbanja, Zlatište*.
(*These areas were under Bosnian Serb control at the time of her writing.) The following names refer to villages and towns elsewhere in Bosnia-Herzegovina:
Bihać**, Bosanski Brod, Bratunac, Čapljina, Foča, Goražde**, Kupres, Mostar, Pale, Šehovići, Srebrenica**, Tuzla**, Višegrad, Zenica, Žepa**.
(**These cities, along with Sarajevo, were declared "safe havens" by the UN.)

Political Background

Chetniks (*četa* = "company," an army unit):
a) Before and during World War I, Serbian irregulars who fought against the Austro-Hungarian and Ottoman armies.
b) During World War II, Serbian royalists under Draža Mihailović, foes of the Ustashas, Partizans, and Nazis (though accused of collaboration with these last).
c) In the present war, Serbian irregulars, especially those loyal to radical nationalist Vojislav Šešelj, fighting against Croatian and Bosnian government forces and engaged in ethnic cleansing; identifiable by their long beards and long knives and by their use of the traditional Serbian crest: the double-headed Byzantine eagle with the Cyrillic slogan CCCC (*Samo Sloga Srbina Spašava* = Only Unity Saves the Serb).
d) By extension, all the Serb forces opposing the Croats and Bosnians, or more generally, all Serbs who support the policies of Karadžić and Milošević (Elma uses the term in all these senses except a).

Ustashas (from the word for "revolt," "uprising"):
a) In World War II, radical Croat nationalists who supported Ante Pavelić's NDH government, a Nazi puppet state: fascist, racist, and genocidal. It was responsible for the death of tens (or hundreds) of thousands of Serbs,

Jews, Gypsies, etc., in Jasenovac concentration camp.

b) Elma uses it as a derogatory term for Croat nationalists who desire the partition of Bosnia-Herzegovina between Croatia and Serbia.

Partizans:
In World War II, the Communist resistance, led by Josip Broz (a.k.a. Tito).

Yugoslavia (= "land of the South Slavs"):
a) From 1919 to 1941, the "Kingdom of Serbs, Croats, and Slovenes" ruled by King Alexander of the Serbian Karađorđević dynasty.

b) From 1945 to 1989, the Socialist Federal Republic of Yugoslavia, a non-aligned communist state led by Marshal Tito and characterized by its economic policy of "workers' self-management" and its ruthless suppression of nationalist movements.

c) From 1992 on, the rump state consisting of the republics of Serbia and Montenegro and the autonomous regions of Vojvodina and Kosovo-Metohija.

Bosnian Muslims:
Serbo-Croatian-speaking inhabitants of Bosnia-Herzegovina and western Serbia (the Sandžak region), descendants of South Slavs (perhaps Bogomil heretics) who converted to Islam during the (Turkish) Ottoman occupation of Bosnia (1463 to 1878). In an impossible position in World War II, they fought on all sides: a few for the Chetniks, some for the Partizans, others for the Ustashas, some even for the Nazis in the "Handžar" SS Division. Considered by Croat and Serb nationalists as being renegade Catholics or Orthodox, respectively, they were finally acknowledged as a separate nationality in the revised Yugoslav constitution of 1974. They have, both historically and in the present war, been on better terms with the Croats than with the Serbs.

Bosnia-Herzegovina *(Bosna i [=and] Herzegovina, BiH):*
Formerly one of the six republics of the Yugoslav federation; now an independent, formally recognized state, although almost 70% of its territory is under the control of the Serb Republic of Bosnia. Its capital is Sarajevo. In

the 1991 census, its population of 4,365,000 was 44% Muslim, 32% Serb, and 17% Croat (5.5% identified themselves only as Yugoslavs). Herzegovina is the predominantly Croat southwestern region. The name Bosnia is often used (incorrectly but understandably) to refer to the whole area.

Serbia:
The largest republic of the former Yugoslavia, now the dominant member of the rump state of the same name. Its capital is Belgrade, which was also the capital of SFR Yugoslavia. Ethnic Serbs constituted 40% of the total population of the former Yugoslavia.

Serb Republic of Bosnia:
An unofficial breakaway republic of BiH, with its capital and parliament in Pale, seventeen kilometres east of Sarajevo.

Serb Republic of Krajina:
An unofficial breakaway republic of Croatia, with its capital in Knin. The Krajina (="region") was before 1878 a military buffer zone between the area of Croatia under Austro-Hungarian rule and Ottoman-controlled Bosnia. The Serbian population of the area was settled there by the Austro-Hungarians to keep the Turks at bay.

Community of Herceg-Bosna:
A short-lived Croat "republic" in western Herzegovina declared by Mate Boban in early 1993 and absorbed into a federative union with Bosnia-Herzegovina in early 1994.

UNPROFOR (United Nations Protection Force):
UN troops with a mandate to ensure the delivery of humanitarian aid to civilians of all nationalities in the former Yugoslavia.

UNHCR (United Nations High Commission for Refugees):
Chosen by the UN to be the lead agency for its humanitarian relief operations in the former Yugoslavia.

Slobodan Milošević:

President of Serbia and *de facto* leader of rump Yugoslavia. His agenda has evidently been the unification of all regions occupied by Serbs into a "Greater Serbia." As of mid-1995, this would include 30% of Croatia and 70% of Bosnia-Herzegovina.

Radovan Karadžić:

President of the Serb Republic of Bosnia, currently wanted by the International War Crimes Tribunal.

Alija Izetbegović:

President of Bosnia-Herzegovina, leader of the SDA (Party for Democratic Action), and a practising Muslim.

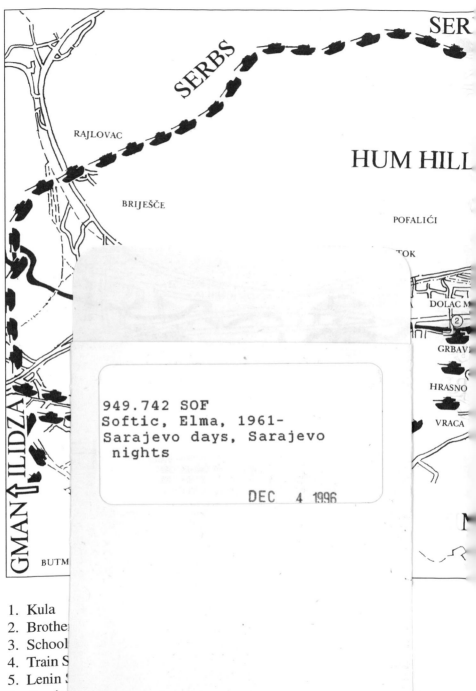

SER

SERBS

SERBS

RAJLOVAC

HUM HILL

BRIJEŠĆE

POFALIĆI

ᵀOK

DOLAC M

②

GRBAV

HRASNO

VRACA

ILIDZA

GMAN ↑ ILIDZA

BUTM

1. Kula
2. Brothe
3. School
4. Train S
5. Lenin S
6. Osmic